Susan Annette Muto

APPROACHING THE SACRED

An Introduction to Spiritual Reading

Susan Annette Muto

APPROACHING THE SACRED

An Introduction to Spiritual Reading

With a Foreword by
Adrian van Kaam

DIMENSION BOOKS
Denville, New Jersey 07834

Published By DIMENSION BOOKS
Denville, New Jersey

Copyright © 1973 by Susan Annette Muto

Grateful acknowledgment is made to the Paulist Press for permission to quote from the Newman Press edition of *The Complete Works of Saint John of the Cross,* trans. and ed. E. Allison Peers (Westminster, Maryland: The Newman Press, 1935); to Doubleday & Company, Inc. for permission to quote selected short passages from *The Jerusalem Bible,* Reader's Edition (Garden City, New York: Doubleday & Company, Inc., 1971); and to Harcourt, Brace & Jovanovich, Inc. for permission to quote selected passages from T.S. Eliot's *Ash-Wednesday* in *Selected Poems,* Harbrace Paperbound Library (New York: Harcourt, Brace & World, Inc., 1936) and the *Four Quartets,* A Harvest Book (New York: Harcourt, Brace & World, Inc., 1943).

All Rights Reserved

TABLE OF CONTENTS

Foreword by Adrian van Kaam 5

Acknowledgments 8

Introduction 9

PART ONE
The Art and Discipline of Spiritual Reading

Meditation, Meditative Reading, Spiritual Reading 15
The Spiritual Writer 20
The Spiritual Reader 26
The Master-Disciple Relationship 28
The Sedimented Past 33
Fear of the Master's Message 36
Compulsion to be Current 40
Option for Repetition 45
Crowd Mentality 49
The Union of Likeness 57
The Solitary Bird 59
Soars as High as it is Able 60
Can Endure No Companionship 62
Places Its Beak Against the Wind 64
Has No Definite Color 71
Sings Sweetly 75
Conclusion 77

PART TWO
A Personal Reading of the *Cautions* of John of the Cross

The First Reading 79
The Second Reading 95
The Third Reading 110
The Fourth Reading 126
The Fifth Reading 134
The Sixth Reading 144

Selected Reading List in the Literature of Spirituality ... 165

FOREWORD

by
Adrian van Kaam

This book is modestly entitled *Approaching the Sacred: An Introduction to Spiritual Reading.* The author wants to help us and herself come nearer to God's presence in daily life. She sees spiritual reading as a means to create an inner atmosphere in which God may reveal Himself to us as we are and where we are. This purpose should be kept in mind if we want to profit from her reflective description of spiritual reading. If our interest and attitude coincide with that of the writer, we will not miss the gift a meditative reading of these beautiful pages can bring. When our aim is to approach the Holy, we are not at that moment interested in scientific exegesis or literary criticism. Such scholarly approaches have their rightful place among those we can take to an author like John of the Cross. However, when we read St. John, or any spiritual writer, in order to grow in intimacy with God, our approach should be of a different nature.

As Dr. Muto explains in the first part of her book, there is to be in this case no critical concentration on the literary or exegetical problems of the text. We let that kind of reading rest for other times and other purposes. Different questions emerge. Is there something in this writing that an average reading like myself can grasp without too much study — something that makes sense to me at this moment? How can I take that meaning out of the book and apply it to my daily life? Am I able to reflect quietly before God on what the text is telling me? Do I allow this writing to gather together my dispersed experiences, enriching them with a new depth of meaning?

At first sight doing the kind of spiritual reading that ties in with daily life seems easy enough. And it would be, if we were able to approach the text with a kind of pristine innocence. Unfortunately, man today is not an innocent reader. He is highly sophisticated, often overly analytical and competitive, intent on having the last word. We must work, therefore, to establish in ourselves a second, enlightened naivety, a style of reading that enables us to leave our sophistication and expertise periodically behind when we want to be present in simplicity and humility to the words of a spiritual master.

Dr. Muto tells us how to establish this second naivety and how to dispose ourselves to the possible emergence of the Sacred in and through those words of the spiritual writer that happen to touch us as we are here and now. She also presents us with a series of living and touching examples of her own way of

Foreword

spiritual reading. We are most grateful that she allows us to share these intimate experiences.

Dr. Muto is eminently qualified for the writing of this book. She holds a doctorate in English Literature with a specialization in the literature of Reformation spirituality and wrote an original and highly regarded dissertation on Milton's *Paradise Lost* in the light of Paul Ricoeur's hermeneutic approach to the symbolism of evil. As assistant director of the Center for the Study of Spirituality of the Institute of Man at Duquesne University, she has been involved with faculty and students in the study and development of a fundamental or foundational Catholic spirituality.

What qualifies her more specifically for this writing is her teaching of graduate courses in this Center on the art and discipline of meditative reflection and spiritual reading. Growing excellence in this field has made her a sought after speaker on these and related topics. Being a modern dynamic laywoman, with a variety of interests and occupations, her writing and reflections are relevant not only for people in religious life but also and especially for numerous men and women in the world who want to live lives of greater depth, humanly and spiritually.

Acknowledgments

I hope in this book to share with you my own love for spiritual reading. I have tried while writing it to grow in the appreciation and practice of this art. The first part looks into spiritual reading as art and discipline; the second part is a series of personal reflections on the first few *Cautions* of John of the Cross. I've written the book in this order, but it need not be read that way. If you prefer, you can read Part One interchangeably with Part Two or Part Two before Part One. Either way is fine. I have also included a reading list of some of my favorite selections from the literature of spirituality.

I am most deeply indebted in this book to the spiritual writings of Fr. Adrian van Kaam. Without the wisdom of his written and spoken words and the benefit of his generous support, this book would not have been written. I am indebted also to my other colleagues at the Center for the Study of Spirituality of the Institute of Man: to Fr. Bert van Croonenburg for his practical advice and patient guidance, to Charles Maes, and to Carolyn Gratton, with whom I have shared fruitful discussions about meditative reflection and spiritual reading. Thanks also to Sr. Margaret Gall, the staff, and the students of our Center for their friendship and support. And a final debt of gratitude to my family.

INTRODUCTION

THE spiritual life is like a plant that grows in a garden. You know how often Jesus spoke of growing things. He said when a seed falls on unfertile soil it is bound to die. When it is planted in good soil it will grow. A beautiful image of the spiritual life. It can die or it can grow. I can say yes to God, but if I don't incarnate this yes in my life, it will weaken, wither, and die.

Jesus was teaching in the cities and towns when someone asked Him who would be saved. He replied, "Try your best to enter by the narrow door, because, I tell you, many will try to enter and will not succeed."[1] I want to go inside that door, but I don't have to. Jesus leaves me free to enter or stay outside. Let's say I choose to go in and follow Him. I may make a lot of mistakes. At times I will fail. I'll have moments of doubt. Do I want to go on? It is not easy to be a follower of Jesus. But I have said yes . . .

I need help if I'm going to make this yes mean something. Help comes to me from God. I can glory in how His grace works through nature. He doesn't destroy. He uplifts. He makes that failing, doubting creature I am the recipient of His word. He is a God who has spoken to His people. He has allowed His word to permeate history, verbally through prophetic preachers and in written form through scribes and spiritual masters. This word has the power to heal my life if I am able to listen.

Spiritual reading is one way to listen to God, yet reading is a most taken for granted act. I read all the time. Road signs and letters from people I love. Magazine articles and books on the best seller list. But how often do I stop and consider the effect of my reading? What happens when and if these words touch my life?

This book is about reading in general and more specifically about spiritual reading. Why should I do spiritual reading? Why not keep my reading confined to books and periodicals about man and the times in which he lives? There are many reasons. By way of introduction, let me cite a few.

Spiritual reading is reading for life at its most profound depths. It is one way to "practice the presence of God" at a time when mankind is making great progress technically but may be regressing in spiritual development. Mankind is in danger of forgetting the Sacred, it is true. Yet there emerge everywhere signs of remembrance. It is the worst of times and the best of times.

Today people desire to meditate. They seek wise men who can teach them how to pray. They crave silent places and turn to nature to heal their hurt. Everywhere appear signs that man wishes to restore

Introduction

his spiritual life. In the words he speaks, in the songs he sings, man desires to recharge this life and its language anew. He wants to experience its fullness again.

Restoring the art of spiritual reading is one way to participate in this call to renewal. Among the various acts of reading I do, spiritual reading ranks the highest. I read to gather the information I need to survive in the world. Newspapers suffice for this purpose. I read to be entertained. A good detective story fills the bill. I read to pursue higher education. Remember those required reading lists in school. And hopefully I do regular spiritual reading, for this act can lead me to the highest human experience of intimacy with the Divine.

Unfortunately, spiritual reading is often neglected. Many days go by when I cannot even squeeze in ten or fifteen minutes. I have all kinds of excuses. I'm busy. There are other books I have to read first. I can't understand what the writer is saying. The Scriptures gather dust on my shelves. The spiritual masters are tucked comfortably away — out of sight, out of mind. Here in the words of Scripture, in the words of spiritual masters, East and West, classic and contemporary, is the help I need to renew my spiritual life. How ironic that the highest act of reading is often the most neglected.

Spiritual reading makes me mindful of the life in me that goes beyond body and ego and seeks its source in God. It awakens me to the call to be nearer to God. Every dimension of my self — emotional, psychological, functional — is destined for this end. To neglect this reading, then, is to neglect a valuable source of self-emergence in presence to the Sacred.

There are other reasons for doing spiritual reading. In a rapidly changing world, the text of the master offers me a testimony to lasting peace. The way is found in a relation to God that surpasses one or the other time bound strife. Christ is the way and presence to Him brings peace. Added to the spiritual master's personal experience of centering in Christ is the tradition and wisdom of the Church and the inspiration of the Holy Spirit. Thus I can take his advice seriously.

Spiritual reading readies me for God's inspiration should He choose to bless me in this way. The text may be the opening through which God speaks to me. In no way is spiritual reading a guarantee that I will become a more spiritual person; such growth is a gift of grace. I cannot predict or control this gift. Done as a mere technique to gain God's favor spiritual reading offers no guarantee; done in humility, in cooperation with God's grace, it can deepen my life.

Spiritual reading helps me to find my true identity before the Father. Of myself I am as nothing in His presence. My everyday self is often a disguise. My true self is hidden in obscurity and nothingness, in direct dependence on God.

The aim of spiritual reading is not to gather

Introduction

information. Its purpose is to release what is deepest in me and what I would like to have access to. I know my spiritual self is there but I cannot get to these depths without some help. Spiritual reading aids me in the discovery of this hidden self. It teaches me where my true homeland lies and reminds me that on earth I am only a pilgrim. In St. Teresa's words, "... it is a great thing to see what is awaiting us there and to know where we are going to live."[2]

The message of the spiritual writer may touch my heart and grant me a gifted moment of inspiration. I cannot read spiritual writing in the same way I read the daily papers. It is more than information; it is invitation. When I read the Gospel alone or with others, I may hear a language that is plaintive, beckoning. These words open up depths and ranges of my personality I never knew existed before I began to dwell upon them.

Living the spiritual life is practically impossible without resourcing myself continually in the words of the spiritual master. These words are an appeal to me from a person who has himself dwelt in silence. Out of his dwelling presence to God has emerged a message for the spiritual life of every man. I can rely on his testimony to lead me to the Eternal. Without this contact, sooner or later I begin to lose inner depth. I find myself becoming busier and busier. Little time is left for bringing myself in recollected presence before the Lord.

Spiritual reading can thus be the starting point

APPROACHING THE SACRED

from which to begin my journey to selfhood and wisdom, a way by which to make uniquely my own the eternal truths all men seek.

PART ONE

The Art and Discipline of Spiritual Reading

THE ART AND DISCIPLINE OF SPIRITUAL READING

Meditation, Meditative Reading, Spiritual Reading

Before I discuss in more detail the ways and means to do spiritual reading, I want to make a few preliminary distinctions, mainly between meditation, meditative reading, and spiritual reading.[1]

Meditation is that period of time I set aside for more personal encounter with Christ. In preparing for my meditation, I may read a few passages from the New Testament to place myself in Our Lord's presence more concretely. Say I want to meditate on Christ's agony in the garden. Something in His response to the suffering He was about to undergo speaks to me of my own desire to listen more faithfully to the Father's will, whatever suffering this may entail.

To prepare for my meditation, I read the appropriate passage in Matthew's Gospel. Then I lay the text aside and try to be present to Christ in Gethsemane, to His simple request that the disciples remain awake, to His acceptance of their human weakness. I stay with Him in loving surrender and at times express my inner feelings.

. . . You suffered this agony for me. You saw my sins and the sins of all mankind, yet You forgave all. How deep is Your love for me. What have I done to merit such mercy? Help me, Lord, to be more deserving . . .

As my time for meditation draws to a close, I may resolve this day to be more compassionate to others in imitation of Christ's compassion for me.

Meditative reading may be considered a variant form of meditation.[2] On occasion it may take the place of mental prayer, but it should not exclusively substitute for it. When I read meditatively, I keep the text in front of me the entire time. This may be a text from Scripture or a passage from a spiritual writer whose work is recognized as a standard source in the literature of spirituality. *The Imitation of Christ* would be a good example.

In this kind of reading, I take a few lines or phrases at a time and then pause to reflect. What is the text saying? How does this saying apply to my life? Following such considerations ought to come the desire to converse with Christ. This conversation may be brief, perhaps lasting only a few minutes. Then I return to the text and continue reading. I pause, reflect, converse, and read again. *How much* I cover is not as important as *how* I cover it. In this way, reading may become an entrance to prayer, which St. Teresa of Avila describes simply as conversation with God.[3]

Spiritual Reading is done outside the time of meditation or meditative reading. It is a foundational discipline of the spiritual life that gives me a frame of reference within which to meet God more personally. Spiritual reading teaches me how to live the truths of Christianity in my day to day life. Time has to be set aside for this reading over and above that spent in meditation.

What kind of spiritual reading should I do during these fifteen minutes or so, a frequently recommended duration, though the length of time for the most part is up to the individual?[4] The first and main source would be Holy Scripture, read not with the aim to meditate upon each sentence but to become more familiar with God's word as speaking in history and through His divine Son. Another source would be the liturgy, read to keep myself in tune with the daily celebration of the Church.

Spiritual reading ought to include the classic works in the literature of Catholic spirituality, like the writings of Augustine, à Kempis, Teresa of Avila, John of the Cross. These works bring to light the fundamental dynamics of the spiritual life. They describe the conditions necessary to predispose myself for this life of intimacy as well as the obstacles I will encounter. They are first hand accounts of one's deepest self, growing in relation to the Divine.

There are also excellent secondary sources related to the primary texts: books on the lives of the saints, descriptions of specific schools of spirituality, accounts of the relationship between active and contemplative life.[5] Some of these books seem to be written with the aim to edify more than to educate, to inspire more than to instruct. This is especially true of the lives of the saints. Still others are written in a less formal vein, more poetic or novelistic. The list of possibilities for spiritual reading is immense. Thus I have to be judicious in my selections.

A few guidelines I've applied in forming my own routine of spiritual reading might be helpful to you. I try first of all to frequent Holy Scripture. This reading strengthens me in the truths of faith. It often speaks directly to my life with and in Our Lord. My next choice would be the spiritual classics. Authors like Thomas à Kempis and Teresa of Avila show me how to live a fundamental Catholic spirituality rooted in the doctrine of the Church. Their ways to reach intimacy with God have met the test of time. I can trust what they tell me and try to live it in accordance with my state of life.

If I begin with the classics, my chances of developing a healthy critical sense in regard to contemporary sources are better than if I read only recent books and make these my standard. In other words, I prefer to judge contemporary works on basis of my reading in the classics and not vice versa. Lacking the critical sense that comes from being rooted in the classics, I might go off in a direction less conducive to balanced spiritual growth and less in tune with the lived teachings of the Church. So I personally enjoy a return to the classic works of Catholic spirituality and am happy to see that many editions are being reissued.[6]

My reading also includes some supportive secondary and explanatory texts. A few that come readily to mind are Evelyn Underhill's books on mysticism, Jean-Baptist Chautard's *The Soul of the Apostolate,* G. K. Chesterton's biography of St. Francis of Assisi. Many fine texts are also available from the Reformation spiritual writers, authors like John Donne, George Herbert, the Quakers, George Fox and John Woolman, and closer to our time Søren Kierkegaard and Dag Hammarskjöld. More contemporary spiritual writings would include books by Thomas Merton and Adrian van Kaam, T. S. Eliot and Nikos Kazantzakis. I've tried to indicate some favorite readings of mine in the list at the end of this book.

Rather than focus primarily on the *what* of spiritual reading, I am more interested in speaking about the *how.* I'll be considering mainly the how of spiritual reading, though many of the obstacles and aids to this kind of reading apply to meditative reading as well.

Let us say as a first guideline to spiritual reading that my approach should not be violent, grasping, manipulative, or upset. I must try to become more tranquil and serene, less agitated and in a rush, more willing to return to a text rich in meaning again and again. Relaxed, I must yet be a most diligent reader. Reading widely, I must yet exercise a certain selectivity. I have to find the books that speak to me and stay with them, not feel guilty if I am unable to read the ten authors on my list. It is better to stay with one, like St. John, and really be there than to read ten and forget what I have read. Patient *staying with* — whether or not I get noticeably "good" results — deepens my powers of concentration even in "dryness" and is an aid to meditation and meditative reading.

Throughout this book, as I dwell on the words of John of the Cross, I hope you will experience as I have that reading can be an avenue to spiritual awakening. Let's begin by taking a brief look at the spiritual writer and then talking about my approaches and problems as a reader.

The Spiritual Writer

John of the Cross is a gifted writer. He has the talent to tell me what he experienced in graced moments of Divine intimacy. This message in turn carries implications for my life. The same is true when I read Scripture or any deeply spiritual text.

The Art and Discipline of Spiritual Reading

This reading makes demands on me to be myself in the deepest sense — the self that I am called to be in presence to God.

To understand what I mean, let's look first at what St. John says. He speaks about what takes place in the contemplative center where self is united with God. To Doña Ana de Peñalosa he writes:

> I have felt some unwillingness, most noble and devout lady, to expound these four stanzas which you have requested me to explain, for they relate to things so interior and spiritual that words commonly fail to describe them, since spirit transcends sense and it is with difficulty that anything can be said of the substance thereof. For it is hard to speak of that which passes in the depths of the spirit if one have not deep spirituality; wherefore, having little thereof myself, I have delayed writing until now. But now that the Lord appears to have opened knowledge somewhat to me and given me some fervour ... I have taken courage, knowing for certain that out of my own resources I can say naught that is of any value, especially in things of such sublimity and substance.[7]

In his writings, St. John attempts to describe the experience of God's self-communication in the center of the soul. At its sublime heights, this experience exceeds all human words. The most eloquent soul falls silent in this "sweet breathing, full of blessing and glory."

Of that breathing of God I should not wish to speak, neither do I desire now to speak; for I see clearly that I cannot say aught concerning it, and that, were I to speak of it, it would seem less than it is. For it is a breathing of God Himself, wherein, in that awakening of lofty knowledge of the Deity, the Holy Spirit breathes into the soul in proportion to the knowledge wherein He most profoundly absorbs it in the Holy Spirit, inspiring it with most delicate love for Himself according to that which it has seen; for, the soul being full of blessing and glory, the Holy Spirit has filled it with goodness and glory, wherein He has inspired it with a love for Himself which transcends all description and all sense, in the deep things of God. And for that reason I leave speaking of it here.[8]

From the start, St. John knows that no matter how talented a writer he is, he will never be able to record in the limited vehicle of words the full depth of his experience. When he does write, there is to be in these words no "worldly rhetoric," no "loquacity and arid eloquence." They will speak to the heart and be bathed in the "sweetness and love" that pleases God. Such words will be "of discretion for the journeyer, of light for the journey and of love for the journeying."[9] St. John seems here to echo St. Paul's words in the first letter to the Corinthians.

As for me, brothers, when I came to you, it was not with any show of oratory or philosophy, but simply to tell you what God has guaranteed. During my stay with you, the only knowledge I claimed to have was about Jesus, and only about him as the crucified Christ. Far from relying on any power of my own, I came among you in great "fear and trembling" and in my speeches and the sermons that I gave, there were none of the arguments that belong to philosophy; only a demonstration of the power of the Spirit. And I did this so that your faith should not depend on human philosophy but on the power of God.[10]

In this relation of intimacy between the writer and God, there is no place for "ingenious human wisdom." There is only the simple and single-minded love of God that then overflows in written words.

This experience evoked in the spiritual writer a sense of mission. To be an instrument of the Divine Will among men, he must try to make this ineffable experience concrete. He knows all the while he writes that words ultimately fail to describe what only silence can contain. Still he feels flooded with new life, with hope and the deep, unshakeable conviction that God is near.

> Moreover, O my God and my delight, my soul has desired, for love of Thee, to employ itself in these sayings of light and love for Thee, for, although I have the tongue wherewith to utter them, I have neither the deeds nor the virtue which pertain to them, and it is with these, my Lord, that Thou art pleased rather than with the language and the wisdom of them. Let other persons. who may be so impelled by them, perchance

make progress in Thy love and service, wherein I am lacking, and let my soul find an occasion of comfort in having been the cause for which Thou findest in others that which is lacking in itself.[11]

In this writing, St. John is comparable to the prophet, often called by God against his will, to tell of these hidden bonds between the temporal and the eternal. That God has chosen him to be His messenger fills the writer with a sense of unworthiness, though for God's sake, he will try to tell others of the love that has enkindled his soul.

Writing of such depth is an act of faith. The writer disposes himself in meekness and fidelity to be an instrument of God's will. It is secondly an act of hope. He hopes that others, with God's grace, may read and profit from what he writes. He has no control over what his words will produce in others, how they will interpret them. Thus the best advice he can give to them is this: '... read these words again, and then perhaps you will cease to doubt, for what I have said is the substance of the truth, and I cannot possibly enlarge upon it here any further."[12] His writing is finally an act of charity that calls him to serve mankind by creating works of mystical truth and beauty, rooted in Divine Scripture and the "sound sense and doctrine of our Holy Mother the Catholic Church."[13]

With faith, hope and love, he crosses the boundary

from the unsayable to the said, from the invisible to the visible. He moves steadily from the realm of silence to the expressive dimension. Through his words, God is able to enter the world anew and I in turn may go to God through the power of the written word. St. John says that what he writes may not be directly understood by my rational intellect; it can, however, move my heart according to the manner and measure of my love for God.

> Since these Stanzas, then, have been composed under the influence of a love which comes from abounding mystical understanding, they cannot be fairly expounded, nor shall I attempt so to expound them, but only to throw upon them some light of a general kind ... And this I think to be best, for sayings of love are better left in their fullness, so that everyone may pluck advantage from them according to his manner and to the measure of his spirit, than abbreviated in a sense to which not every taste can accommodate itself. And thus, although they are expounded after a certain manner, there is no reason why anyone should be bound to this exposition. For mystical wisdom (which comes through love, whereof the present Stanzas treat) needs not to be understood distinctly in order to produce love and affection in the soul; it is like to faith, whereby we love God without understanding Him.[14]

The spiritual writer is not stopped by lack of rational proof for what he sees. By the inner urge of love, he is compelled to communicate his experience to others. By an act of faith, he follows the inspiration of grace wherever it leads and in the end returns to his fellow men bearing the good news of hope and salvation. The question is, will I be ready to hear his message?

With this question in mind, I want to consider ways of preparing myself to become a better spiritual reader. What obstacles block my capacity to listen? What conditions facilitate its development? Exploring such questions will hopefully clarify the best approach to spiritual reading.

The Spiritual Reader

In trying to live a spiritual life, many obstacles emerge. To tell me what these are and how, with God's grace, I can overcome them is one task of the spiritual writer. In his following of Christ, he discovered ways to bring the Lord into the day to day routine of life. In revealing these ways, he does not give me an easy lesson in how to solve the problems of society. Rather he writes about becoming a more prayerful person.

Within the same work he may pierce to the depths of despair and frustration as well as sing of the heights of ecstasy and freedom. He is open to people, things, and events as manifestations of the Divine. Rather than isolate one dimension of reality as ultimate, he works steadily for a deepening integration. He avoids one-sided concentration on either

The Art and Discipline of Spiritual Reading

persons, things, or events. Seeing all against the horizon of the Sacred, he tries instead to reach a new synthesis of self, others, and situation in God.

The dynamics of experience the sacred writer uncovers are common to all men in search of the Holy. His writing is not an ancient artifact to be admired but a current message to be assimilated. Its main purpose is to awaken the spirit in me. He reminds me that I am always in danger of losing my deeper interiority. He calls me back to the priorities of spiritual living that must permeate my day to day existence. He tells me how to live in utmost surrender to the will of God, even if doing His will makes me a mockery in the eyes of men. Listening to Him brings peace.

The word of the sacred writer is never a closed door; it is an open window. Through it I see all creation playing before the face of the Father. In awe I witness words that reveal untold mysteries of life. They open me to the secret that I am. I am present to reality not only in its immediate appearances — to what eye can see and hand can touch — but to the meaning behind these appearances and ultimately to their deepest ground and origin.

To ready myself to hear these most profound messages, I have to devote time to the preparation of myself as spiritual reader. I cannot say I am prepared to do spiritual reading because I know how to read or have had some courses in the history of spirituality.

Spiritual reading, like the spiritual life, involves more than technical know-how.

The Master-Disciple Relationship

> He that desires to be alone, without the support of a master and guide, will be like the tree that is alone in the field and has no owner. However much fruit it bears, passers-by will pluck it all, and it will not mature.[15]
>
> The soul that is alone and without a master, and has virtue, is like the burning coal that is alone. It will grow colder rather than hotter.[16]

In these sentences, St. John speaks of the disciple without a master. It becomes clear upon further reading that he is not thinking of a specific human master but rather of Christ the Master. Christ is the first spiritual master. He is available to me at all times and in all places. Even when good direction is not to be had, spiritual growth is possible if I place myself under obedience to Christ's teaching word. Not having the "right" person is no excuse for not advancing in the spiritual life.

Clearly, when I consider the human spiritual master, I see he does not possess autonomous power. The true master recognizes himself as a mere channel of grace. He knows that he does not convert the initiate. It is God who calls and grants the gift of Himself to the soul ready to receive Him. I do not necessarily need a spiritual master to meet God, but if

The Art and Discipline of Spiritual Reading

a wise, experienced and humble person is available all the better.[17]

Spiritual reading presupposes this relation of master to disciple. The path to God is opened to me in texts of spiritual writers recognized by the Church. When I do spiritual reading, the text, as it were, is the master; I am the disciple. The text as master becomes the ground of truth that prevents my reading from becoming too subjectivistic. Only when I affirm the truths articulated in the text, am I free to appropriate them in my personal life. Otherwise I may falsify the message of the master.

In the parallel of "text to master," the text conveys a way of life I as disciple am eager to assimilate. The text is to me what the master is to the disciple, a guide for one who is on the way. Disciple in this sense means disciplined listener. The master has found and followed those paths that lead most readily to the Divine. He has recorded his gathered wisdom in spiritual treatises and sayings. In his words, I as disciplined listener may discover what I must do to awaken myself to the presence of God within me.

My task as reader is to discipline myself in such a way that the needs and strivings of my emotional self, my prejudices and romantic feelings, do not take over. An awakening to my deepest self is facilitated if I place myself at the disposal of the master in the words he speaks. I want not to lead but to be led, not to tell but to listen, not to transform but to be transformed. Mine is a receptive rather than an aggressive stance. My desire is to follow with docility. Not to negate but to affirm. Not to find fault with the master's words but to allow them to find fault with me.

The master may not have all the answers I seek but he is able to witness to what it is like to live in presence to the Lord. To share this experience, I must quiet my analytical mind, surrender my problem solving mentality, my competitive thinking, and begin to live in the wonder of not knowing, of not being there but of being on the way. The attitude of wonder is one way of disciplining myself so I can listen to the secret wisdom of the spiritual writer.

Say I am at the shore. I feel small and insignificant as a grain of sand before the vast horizon of sea and sky that stretches before me. No sound reaches me but the incessant roar of waves exploding on the shore. All this vastness and me. Cares loosen their grip. Woes release their frantic clutch. It may happen suddenly that things fall in place: who I am, why I am here, where I am going. Wonder takes me out of my narrow self and relates me to a higher order of things. I feel whole. The tension drains out of me. I give silent thanks for the mystery, and now momentary clarity, of my human condition. Though finite and limited, I am infinitely loved. Someone remembers me, as He remembers each grain of sand at my feet, each wispy cloud above my head.

The Art and Discipline of Spiritual Reading

This sense of wonder binds me to the whole and Holy. It heightens my inner peace and restores the possibility of disciplined listening. My thoughts find a new center of truth: that which is greater than I, that in which I live and move and have my being.

The spiritual writer often evokes in me the wonder of admiration. The beauty of nature and the blessing of God on all created things fills me with gratitude. The wonder of admiration awakens joy. At other times, as master of paradox, the writer may evoke in me the wonder of puzzlement. The text brings to light truths that seem strange to reason while describing faithfully what is going on in experience.

I read in Scripture many examples that elicit the wonder of puzzlement. In God's eyes, for example, my weakness may really be strength when it signifies my need for Him; my strength only weakness when it manifests proud self-reliance. Our Lord relates parables that tell how the first shall be last, and the last first; how the proud shall be humbled, and the humble exalted. Such spiritual paradoxes are to be meditated upon, not in a cerebral way that is busy and rambling but in a prayerful mood that is receptive and imbibing. Mental grasping of the message has to give way to the living experience of this word.

The task before me is not to solve the paradox with my reasoning intellect but to live it experientially as the meaning of this mystery begins to emerge, to dwell on the text, to let its meaning penetrate me so that it becomes part of the living pattern of my life. Once I "see" with eyes of faith what the spiritual text means, I can begin to form my life according to its directives. I can let its message become truth *for me* — however strange my stance may appear to reason.

> The language of the cross may be illogical to those who are not on the way to salvation, but those of us who are on the way see it as God's power to save ... If it was God's wisdom that human wisdom should not know God, it was because God wanted to save those who have faith through the foolishness of the message that we preach. And so, while the Jews demand miracles and the Greeks look for wisdom, here are we preaching a crucified Christ; to the Jews an obstacle that they cannot get over, to the pagans madness, but to those who have been called, whether they are Jews or Greeks, a Christ who is the power and the wisdom of God. For God's foolishness is wiser than human wisdom, and God's weakness is stronger than human strength.[18]

I can never plumb the mystery of God's wisdom. It fills me with wonder. Without knowing how it happens, the text shimmers with meaning. I can spend long hours dwelling on these words and never exhaust the range of experience they communicate about the Christian life. What would it profit me to know intellectual truths about God and forget my personal call to transcendence, where I am nothing

The Art and Discipline of Spiritual Reading

and He is all. More and more, through meditative reading, presence to the Divine may permeate all I am and do. Each time I read such texts in a loving way, they may yield a deeper dimension of meaning, if I have grown in my capacity to listen.

In a more specific way, then, I want to explore a few of the personal and cultural obstacles that may block my capacity as a disciple to listen to the words of the spiritual master. Later on, I will try to describe the conditions that facilitate spiritual awakening and a dwelling approach to the text. First, some personal obstacles.

The Sedimented Past

To read the spiritual master and hear what he is saying about my life, I must try to bring to light the prejudices, emotions, and assumptions of my past that may make it impossible for me to listen quietly These sediments of the past are less likely to get in the way of the text's address to my life in the present if I am able to do this work of uncovering.

A first obstacle to spiritual reading is thus my inability to "let go" of the sedimented past. It is true that I cannot get rid of my past. It is a part of me. My present act of reading is conditioned by my family history, education, and life style up to this moment. I bring my whole self to my reading of the spiritual text. Still I have to recognize in myself parts of me that have become, in regard to spiritual reading, points of closure to the words of the master. The best way of recognizing these is to think of red flags going up.

Sedimented in my past, for example, may be an unworked through dislike of anything that smacks of tradition. For me freedom means throwing off the dust of the past and damning any structure over ten years old as hopelessly obsolete. A red flag goes up when mention is made of the age old need for solitude, silence, detachment, and surrender of my pet desires.

Such a stereotyped reaction makes it impossible for me to hear the truths of the master that are transtemporal and speak to every generation. If I am unable to "let go" of my blind rebellion toward tradition, I may lose my best chance to be transformed. I need to discover through my reading and the way I listen to speakers what is my profile of one-sidedness. Once I discover my patterns of closure, I am less likely to miss these transtemporal messages.

In this way, what is an obstacle to spiritual reading and life, namely, stereotyped prejudice, can be an aid in disguise if I explore it in the proper way. It is helpful to know what I can or cannot listen to and why. I need to recognize such prejudices and try to overcome them so I can ready myself for God's self-revelation in the present. Such honest self-examination may be the beginning of growth in a more positive direction.

When I do discover a pattern of closure, the answer is not to go to the opposite extreme of total openness. Being open to everything means in effect being committed to nothing. I do stand somewhere and it is good to be open to what spontaneously attracts and repels me. Many times a "gut" reaction is more to be trusted than a rationalized response. I ought to listen to my feelings of alienation or enthusiasm, like or dislike, and try to discern what they are really telling me about myself. In short, I must try to avoid both extremes: instant dislike or instant affirmation. Enthusiasm for what the writer is saying can be genuine, but it may also mean that I like only what I agree with already.

The answer to patterns of closure is not total openness but thoughtful concern. Let me be thoughtful about what I feel. Faith that the writer has something of value to say must precede any disbelieving tendency to dismiss his words. This dismissal may come with flat negation. An even more subtle dismissal is that of "aesthetic appreciation." I affirm how much I enjoy what the writer is saying but carefully avoid letting him touch my life. As long as I maintain the attitude of "spectator upon," I am still in the stance of closure, however aesthetic my form of resistance may be.

Let me try to open myself to the text in an honest way, examining these patterns of closure and working them through. In this way, I may discover how well the experience recorded in the text illumines, deepens, or refines my own.

Fear of the Master's Message

Fear of the implications of the master's message — if I take it seriously — is another personal obstacle to listening. As a starting point to illustrate this obstacle, let's consider what St. John says regarding "pleasure in sensible objects."

> Furthermore, this desire leads such persons into great inconstancy. Some of them never continue in one place or even always in one state: now they will be seen in one place, now in another; now they will go to one hermitage, now to another; now they will set up this oratory, now that. Some of them, again, wear out their lives in changing from one state or manner of living to another. For, as they possess only the sensible fervour and joy to be found in spiritual things, and have never had the strength to attain spiritual recollection by the renunciation of their own will, and submitting to suffering inconveniences, whenever they see a place which they think well suited for devotion, or any kind of life or state well adapted to their temperament and inclination, they at once go after it and leave the condition or state in which they were before. And, as they have come under the influence of that sensible pleasure, it follows that they soon seek something new, for sensible pleasure is not constant, but very quickly fails.[19]

Especially if I have given into the tendency to seek the new, the spectacular, the out of the ordinary in prayer, a normal fear emerges if I take this text seriously. St. John deflates the importance I have attached to feelings in prayer and suggests that I try to settle down in spiritual recollection. Unless feelings diminish their hold on me, I may become too concerned with myself and with what *I* must feel and do to meet God. I may try out all kinds of new prayer experiments, each one of which gives me a different feeling. If I am an ardent seeker after the new — and all of us are in part because of our cultural situation — I may resist the directive to be still. I may be afraid not to "feel." I am afraid especially if I have made these feelings an ultimate concern. What if I take what he says seriously? I may have to give up my latest experiments and return to the ordinary prayers of the Church to get my bearings.

Other fears may emerge as I read further in St. John. Spiritual living calls for childlike faith in Christ; I fear the risk. Loving God demands uncompromising surrender; I fear the consequences. I must give all to God; yet how I fear an unconditional yes to the Father's will. All these fears of mine are really "ego" fears, that is, fears rooted in my self-centeredness. They are not related to the healthy fear of the Lord that is the beginning of wisdom, the sense of His awesome power and my nothingness. Ego fears emerge because I may have to give up my old ways. I wanted to tell God what to do. Now I have to stop talking and try to listen.

If I live in fear of listening, my style of hearing is

likely to remain critical and fault-finding. I force the text to fit my standards. I cannot resist the tendency to "grind my own ax." I interpret the text; I do not allow it to interpret me.

If I reflect on this obstacle, as I reflected on the sedimented past, it may become an aid to spiritual living. When I am afraid of something, it is natural to be on the defensive. Fear of being wrong immediately puts me on guard. I fear the truth of what is being said and try to avoid it. So I read the text like a trial lawyer preparing his defense. Only the sad thing is, if I win the case, I really lose. I may be able to outwit the spiritual master by intellectual repartee but what will I have gained? What good is the last word if saying it jeopardizes my soul?

I need to catch myself when I become defensive, when I begin to build systems of rationalization against a text that does not slide neatly into my way of thinking. Instead of defensiveness, I need to renew my receptivity. Receptivity is not passivity, for I am in dialogue with the text all the time. My relation to the writer's message is one of active passivity and passive activity. Both sides must exist simultaneously.

As a disciplined reader, I bring to the text a whole self, involved in many responsibilities. When I begin to read the sacred text, I need first to discipline this active self by quieting it down, by making it passive, by opening it to the words and wisdom of the master. On this side my relation to the text is one of active passivity. At the same time, it is one of passive activity. I have to do something with what I receive. The word has to be embodied in daily life. So when I read, the two sides have to come together. I listen and receive; I speak and am spoken to.

Reading is like peeling an onion. One layer is stripped away only to reveal another until finally I reach the core. In this quiet peeling, God takes the initiative. Reaching this core experience of presence to Him is the goal of spiritual reading, but it will not happen without God's grace. I cooperate with this grace by approaching the text in a spiral way. Each time I listen closely a new layer of meaning may be revealed, for such is the unending richness of the spiritual word.

Such reading requires that I do not let a "first reading fear of the text" turn me off. Instead I return to the text and try to enter into the spirit in which these words were written, opening myself to the layers of meaning that lie beneath the veneer of style and historical circumstance.

A good example of the power of the spiritual word to speak to the proper listener is found in St. Bernard's sermons on the Song of Songs.[20] He went back to the spiritual canticle again and again and each time drew out of it a new depth of meaning. The text yielded its richness to the degree that he was able to bring himself before it in an ever deepening mood of humility and reflective participation. Each time he approached the text he brought with him all that he had learned from his prior readings; he brought also his own rich life of prayer up to that point. Then he allowed the text to "educate" him further. That is, he allowed the text to "lead" him on to greater intimacy with the Divine. The text became his teacher in a sense; he became the disciple of the text and attempted to take in bit by bit the wisdom of its message. In this way, the text led him out of himself and nearer to God. He had ears to hear and, with God's guidance, he heard what the text had to reveal. In turn he wrote many sermons, attempting to nourish others with the spiritual food he had received from reading the Song of Songs.

The fear I feel toward what the text is saying is thus cast out by perfect love. Love leads me back to the text a second and a third time. These words can reorient my life, if I am able to overcome my personal fears for resisting them.

Compulsion to be Current

Being current is to a certain extent indispensable for life in the modern world. Is being current a danger to the spiritual life? No, except when this urge to be current becomes a compulsion. I have to know what is going on, but the question is, can I do so without losing inner peace? Simply avoiding current issues is not the answer. I must learn how to be current while at the same time fostering growth in the spiritual life

The Art and Discipline of Spiritual Reading

by returning to my inner self and to the writings of spiritual masters whose words about the way to God have withstood centuries of change. By rooting myself in the basic truths of faith, I can be current without being swept away by changing events.

Though mass media does serve the public good, privately it often has the effect of pulling me outside of myself. It is practically impossible, when out in public, to distance myself from the news media. People walk by with radios blaring. Corner newsboys blast the headlines. Every bar boasts its own TV. In the privacy of my home, I can choose on occasion to distance myself from this bombardment, but the problem of public media is not merely a matter of turning the television off.

Aside from the fact that in general people read less because they watch television more, the spiritual life is endangered by the kind of listening the media calls me to. This is a listening mainly with my outer informational ear instead of with my inner meditative ear. The outer ear suffices when I listen to the six o'clock news, but it is not sharp enough to hear the profound messages communicated by the spiritual masters.

When Our Lord said that those who have ears to hear will hear, He meant those able to listen with the ears of the inner man. Many who heard His words only listened to them in an external way. He was dubbed by them a poor politician, a bad economist, an outright fool. Persons who lacked an inner ear, because they lacked an inner life, could listen only to the outward sense of His message, and to the outer ear He often talked nonsense. When I close my inner ear to the message of the Gospel, it is as if I put a veil over myself and prevent the clarity of the spiritual word from illuminating my soul.

More than ever today I am in danger of listening with my outer ear alone. This danger is great because of the vast array of information beamed at me every minute by the media. The technological society tempts me to live on a superficial level. I collect tidbits of information about this and that, seldom stopping to recollect myself. Little wonder that my inner ear atrophies. Gradually it loses its power to listen. The outer informational ear takes over. It has many sources of nourishment: television, radio, newspapers, billboards, magazines, and the many new books I have to read if I want to stay current. The outer ear has to be "in the know," "up to date with the latest." Its favorite phrase is "Have you heard?" or "Did you know?"

Again without denying the necessity of being up to date in accordance with my situation, I must do inspirational reading of spiritual masters even though this may mean missing some of the flow of information. I am in the world and must be part of that world. However, the danger is that I may become so involved in what I'm doing that I neglect the call of

The Art and Discipline of Spiritual Reading

the inner life. I hear only the call toward what is the latest.

The conditions that facilitate listening with the inner ear are often opposite those for the outer. The inner ear hears best in silence. Instead of the compulsion to be current, it has the desire to dwell. Instead of being in the know, it is content to rest in the cloud of unknowing. Tired quickly by watching TV, the inner ear may thrive on a few sentences from the Psalms.

The great questions facing the person who wants to deepen his spiritual life are these: Can I resist the pull of the culture toward exteriority and follow the inward bent of the spiritual master? Can I read the classic masters not demanding to hear something new but to deepen what I already know?

The answer is not to do away with the outer ear but to moderate its dominance. I can do so by giving my inner ear a chance to listen. Cease being current for a while. Do everyday at least fifteen minutes of spiritual reading.[2][1] Allow room for God's voice to be heard. For how can I listen to His voice in my deepest self if I am always listening to things outside of myself?

A good mood to acquire when I do spiritual reading is the vacation mood. I recall those one or two weeks when I am able to get away from my workaday life. I go off to a house by the shore or a cabin in the woods. "Thank God," I say, "The phones won't ring. The newspapers won't be delivered. The television set is back home." I feel relaxed, no longer entangled in business affairs. I have a chance to be myself.

When I come back from vacation, I find that life has gone on. It's like watching a soap opera. Say I can't get to the story for a month or two. I turn it on one day and the story line picks up right where it left off. Life goes on. So I can cease feeling compelled to crowd every moment with activity. At least when doing spiritual reading, I try to maintain the vacation mood inwardly if not outwardly. This mood leads to simplicity and increases the likelihood of my being able to hear the spiritual master.

Then, too, the vacation mood helps to quiet me down. My body feels more rested. The knots in my stomach begin to untie. And when my body is rested, my mind tends to be more alert. The compulsive tendency, on the other hand, leads to physical and mental exhaustion. To overcome this a calm letting go of the outer is necessary for a while. Patterns of tiredness tell me it is time to retire. Rest for a while. Get away from it all. The media will be there when I return. Be by myself. Take along at most one favorite book. The stuffed feeling of having taken in too much information is a signal to let go, to lead a life bound not only to the outer ear but to the inner ear as well.

Option for Repetition

How does reading the spiritual master help me resist the compulsion to be current? The answer lies in his option for repetition. I am not speaking here of obsessive repetition, the inability to let go of an idea, but repetition in the spiritual sense. This repetition implies a docile re-utterance of the truths of faith contained in Holy Scripture and in the writings of the Fathers and Doctors of the Church. Repetition in this sense is a necessary component of the reflective life. It is the opposite of agitation.

The nature of newness is to breed agitation. Unfamiliarity makes me restless. Custom makes me feel at home. The spiritual master does not foster agitated flitting around. He stands somewhere. When I read his words, I feel tranquil. Mine is the tranquilization that comes from hearing timeless truths repeated again and again. Such repetition is especially comforting in an age which demands that I be current.

The spiritual master knows the truths of the inner life are found in Holy Scripture and in the doctrine, traditions, and mysteries held sacred by the Church and its Magisterium. He witnesses to these trans-temporal truths. This option for repetition is a conscious choice on his part. His task is not to expound novel theories about Revelation but to repeat through the filter of his own experience the principles and dynamics of religious living taught by the Church for ages. On the one hand, he repeats these timeless truths and, on the other, he illumines them anew with the uniqueness of his religious experience.

To illustrate this point, I can select a theme and trace it through several centuries of spiritual writers. The theme will be: "Thy will be done." The first link in the chain is Holy Scripture and the Gospel according to St. John.

> All that the Father gives me will come to me,
> and whoever comes to me
> I shall not turn him away;
> because I have come from heaven,
> not to do my own will,
> But to do the will of the one who sent me.[22]

From here, I go to the sixteenth century and read in the *Living Flame of Love* a description of the highest union of the soul and God:

> So the understanding of the soul is now the understanding of God; and its will is the will of God; and its memory is the memory of God; and its delight is the delight of God; and the substance of the soul, although it is not the Substance of God, for into this it cannot be changed, is nevertheless united in Him and absorbed in Him, and is thus God by participation in God, which comes to pass in this perfect state of the spiritual life, although not so perfectly as in the next life. And in this

way by 'slaying, thou hast changed death into life.' And for this reason the soul may here say very truly with Saint Paul: 'I live, now not I, but Christ liveth in me.' And thus the death of this soul is changed into the life of God, and the soul becomes absorbed in life . . .[23]

This desire for union of my will with the will of God for me is affirmed in the seventeenth century by Sir Thomas Brown. In *Religio Medici,* he offers this as a closing prayer:

> Blesse mee in this life with but the peace of my conscience, command of my affections, the love of thy selfe and my dearest friends, and I shall be happy enough to pity *Caesar*. These are, O Lord, the humble desires of my most reasonable ambition, and all I dare call happinesse on earth: wherein I set no rule or limit to thy hand or providence; dispose of me according to the wisedome of thy pleasure. Thy will bee done, though in my owne undoing.[24]

And finally, in the twentieth century, T. S. Eliot restates in *Ash-Wednesday* what is clearly a transtemporal truth.

> This is the time of tension between dying and birth
> The place of solitude where three dreams cross
> Between blue rocks
> But when the voices shaken from the yew-tree drift away
> Let the other yew be shaken and reply.
> Blessèd sister, holy mother, spirit of the fountain, spirit of the garden,

APPROACHING THE SACRED

> Suffer us not to mock ourselves with falsehood
> Teach us to care and not to care
> Teach us to sit still
> Even among these rocks,
> Our peace in His will
> And even among these rocks
> Sister, mother
> And spirit of the river, spirit of the sea,
> Suffer me not to be separated.
>
> And let my cry come unto Thee.[25]

Each author reflects the style and mode of expression proper to his century. Each is influenced by the cultural and ecclesiastical history of his time; yet each repeats the same truth: "Thy will be done."

When I engage in this exercise of finding thematic links, I develop an historical sense, so necessary for the spiritual life. Chronological time speaks to me of the eternal now of God. Men of every age voice His truths again and again. These truths must be reheard by every generation since each age begins anew the search for eternal life. Eliot for one makes no apology for this work of repetition. History is for him a pattern of timeless moments. It is thus the work of the spiritual master to witness to transtemporal truths.

> You say I am repeating
> Something I have said before. I shall say it again.

Shall I say it again? In order to arrive there,
To arrive where you are, to get from where you are
    not,
    You must go by a way wherein there is no ecstasy.
In order to arive at what you do not know
    You must go by a way which is the way of ignorance.
In order to possess what you do not possess
    You must go by the way of dispossession.
In order to arrive at what you are not
    You must go through the way in which you are not.
And what you do not know is the only thing you know
And what you own is what you do not own
And where you are is where you are not.[26]

Thus the spiritual master is always recognizable by his option for repetition in opposition to the culture's plea for newness. His task, in other words, is not invention but repetition. He repeats within the uniqueness of his own experience the perennial truths of the spiritual life. Reading his words helps bring me to rest and spiritual calm. Repetition of these spiritual truths is the means by which I can become a more disciplined listener to the word of God.

Crowd Mentality

Spiritual reading is a risk because it opens up questions about my life that I may prefer not to reflect upon. Intermingled with this pain is the joy of being reborn in Christ. The question is, am I willing to walk alone down a road that leads to simplicity and possibly to pain? On this road I experience failure and repentance, a growing detachment from myself and my needs. I experience solitude and a lessening of attachment to the thought of what others will think of me. The power of the anonymous "they" diminishes as I discover myself before God. Still I am aware of what a powerful obstacle to spiritual life and reading the crowd mentality can be. Instead of developing an inner life, I allow myself to be carried by the latest tide of opinion. The crowd divides my attention. There is in the crowd the danger of what Aldous Huxley calls "herd intoxication."[27] Such intoxication usually involves exclusive absorption of the self by a group or movement outside of the self. I have such a need to be "in" with others that I close off the call of my deepest self which may be inviting me to stand alone.

I may choose the crowd to escape the pain of loneliness. Banding together with the group absorbs all my time, energy, and effort. I don't have to face myself before God. I may cover up this idolatry of the crowd by saying, "My work with them is prayer" or "The only place I meet God is in them." I can always use "God's will" as a canopy to cover up crowd worship, to hide my fear of standing alone.

Søren Kierkegaard pierces the foolishness of this illusion. In eternity, he says, there are no crowds. Each one becomes an individual.

> The individual is always only one and conscience in its meticulous way concerns itself with the individual. In eternity you will look in vain for the crowd.[28]
>
> You will be asked only whether you may not have ruined the best within you by joining the crowd in its defiance, thinking that you were many and therefore you had the prerogative, because you were many, that is, because you were many who were wrong.[29]

What are my real motivations for being with others? Do I hide my feelings to be in with the latest fad? Am I sufficiently alone or always on the run? I have to come to the point of questioning my life if spiritual reading is to take effect. I have to pause long enough to discover who I am so that reading the sacred writer can reveal who Christ is calling me to become.

I have to be with others but I must never forget that I have a unique stand. This stand may be years in the making, but only if I maintain it can I avoid falling in with the latest whim of the crowd. For the spiritual person, this stand involves humility and self-effacement. More and more I try to empty myself and become an instrument whom God may use as He wills. In whatever situation I find myself, I try to do the Christ-like thing, knowing when to forgive as He forgave, knowing when to "overthrow the money changers in the temple," when to speak and when to be still, when to be alone and when to be with others.

The crowd mentality, unless I work to overcome it, may carry over into my attitude toward community. Instead of regarding community as a supportive arm for the personal and spiritual growth of each member, I may make it a poor substitute for family or friendship.[30] Being all alike, instead of respectfully supporting one another's uniqueness in Christ, may become the standard. The stress is on togetherness often to the exclusion of uniqueness.

Different styles of life within the same community can best be tolerated if behind each person I recognize Christ. It becomes easier to cope with one another's differences when the horizon of community is not merely human but transcendent. Without the faith dimension that posits the presence of Christ in each person, it is easy for the levelling mentality of the crowd to take over. People become objects to be mobilized. The many override the one. The community no longer provides the possibility for spiritual growth; as crowd it becomes an obstacle to this growth.

Communities should instead be places of shared solitude. In order to meet God as God, I must find Him first in solitude. When others find Him in this same way, we have a solid basis for coming together. The truest oneness emerges from the deepest aloneness. Community is the tension between solitude and togetherness. If solitude is overstressed, community may become a glorified hotel where a person eats his

The Art and Discipline of Spiritual Reading

meals and finds a bed but cares little for his neighbor. If solitude is understressed, such fusion may occur that healthy community no longer exists.[31]

A community that values the right amount and kind of solitude gives each member time to be alone with God. The members of the community become guardians of one another's availability to the Sacred through simple acts of supportive togetherness like praying for and with one another, adoration of God in the common prayer of the Church, and frequent periods of spiritual reading.

In this light it is clear that spiritual reading is first of all a solitary act. When properly prepared for, it can be done together, but first, it has to be a personal work. Private spiritual reading does not preclude reading a text together, but communal reading should never replace personal, as is likely to happen if the crowd mentality prevails.

In personal reading, the words of the spiritual master are directed to my deepest self where I stand in solitude before the Sacred. Such reading is best done alone. Why alone? Because in this way I can respect my own pace. I may read five pages while someone else may read fifteen. Spiritual reading is not a matter of quantity but of quality. If I set aside fifteen minutes a day for spiritual reading, I may read only one or two psalms. But if I allow this reading to touch my life, it is much better than reading five psalms and hardly seeing the words on the page because I'm going so fast. Reading five lines of one psalm and letting them speak to me is more inspiring than reading five psalms in their entirety and letting them become merely part of my repertoire of information.

Alone, there is less chance of interference should the Spirit address me through the text.

> Yahweh, our Lord,
> how great your name throughout the earth!
>
> Above the heavens is your majesty chanted
> by the mouths of children, babes in arms.
> You set your stronghold firm against your foes
> to subdue enemies and rebels.
>
> I look up at your heavens, made by your fingers,
> at the moon and stars you set in place —
> ah, what is man that you should spare a thought for him,
> the son of man that you should care for him?[32]

The familiar words of the Eighth Psalm never fail to impress me but one day they strike a new chord. My sister-in-law gives birth to a baby girl. Knowing that God's care hovers over my neice fills me with gratitude. His love shall accompany her in life, as it has me, in spite of my infidelities. Reading this text brings me closer to the Lord and, on this day, I can truly join the psalmist in proclaiming His greatness.

On another day I read, "From the depths I call to you, Yahweh, / Lord, listen to my cry for help!"[33] The cry of a soul in anguish begging God for mercy.

This text spoke to me as never before. I received word that one of my friends died unexpectedly. As I read the words of this psalm, I am able to place myself before God, imploring His kindness for my friend and His mercy for those who mourn him.

It is more the exception than the rule that the text speaks to me in such a powerful way. An ordinary result of spiritual reading is simply a greater awareness of God's goodness, majesty, and love in comparison to my weakness, poverty, and pride. Even this ordinary result may not be noticeable. However much I try to be meaningfully present to the text, days may pass when nothing seems to happen. It's at times like these that I'm tempted to give up or neglect spiritual reading. It doesn't seem to do any good.

Though I may not notice it, perseverance in daily reading slowly, imperceptibly, has its impact on me. As time goes on, I may become more spiritually aware. The goodness and love of God, my dependence on Him, my gratefulness to Him have become more real for me. Daily reading has not been a waste of time after all. Though the results do not show immediately, they are no less real. Compare the watering of a plant. Without faithful watering, the leaves would soon wither. So too the spiritual life. Unless it is properly tended, it will not thrive. Lacking regular encounter with God through spiritual reading, this life loses its strength.

Sometimes it is helpful to read one or the other

passage aloud. I have tried this with certain psalms and found that reading them aloud had a special impact on me. In the privacy of my room the effect seems more powerful if I hear these words echoing back to me in my own voice. They make a deeper impression when I hear them as well as see them. Hearing a song sung is more rewarding than merely reading the lyrics on the record cover. Reading aloud also slows me down. I am less likely to use methods of speed reading that have no place here. Forced to slow down, I am more likely to go back and re-read. While this is not my usual way of doing spiritual reading, at certain times and with certain texts it can be advantageous.

I may keep a notebook beside me and write down messages that mean the most to me. Later I may mediate upon them. In this spiritual reading notebook, I do not focus narrowly on faults and failings in a confessional way. I simply record the words that touch me most and my reflective response to their message. I remember through this writing when God has been there to comfort me in my sorrow, to celebrate with me in my joy. I learn from the rhythm of writing and reading with impedes my growth in spiritual living and similarly what helps to facilitate this growth. Alone in my room, with the text before me and my notebook beside me, I become aware of an inner space, away from the crowd, where God calls me as His own.

The Union of Likeness

In the *Ascent of Mount Carmel,* St. John describes the "substantial union" that exists between the soul and God. God is substantially in me, and this union gives me being. If God's self-willing of me were to cease at any moment, I myself would cease to be.

> ... it must be known that God dwells and is present substantially in every soul, even in that of the greatest sinner in the world. And this kind of union is ever wrought between God and all the creatures, for in it He is preserving their being: if union of this kind were to fail them, they would at once become annihilated and would cease to be.[34]

St. John goes on to say that the purpose of his writing is not so much to describe this substantial union that is mine by the fact that God has created me. Rather he wants to address my attention to the "union of likeness." I grow in unlikeness to God through selfishness; I retain my likeness through selflessness. Present within me is the power to repent and through Christ's redemptive love, the possibility of reunion with God. I become more like God by making my will more and more at one with His will.

> For the whole business of attaining to union with God consists in purging the will from its affections and desires; so that thus it may no longer be a base, human will, but may become a Divine will, being made one with the will of God.[35]

This growth in likeness is a life long endeavor. It is something I must steadily strive after if I want to receive the union of likeness. Grace comes to me as pure gift, but it is a gift I must cooperate with. In the early stages of the spiritual life this cooperation is shown by acts of purification and discipline that awaken me to a sense of utter dependency on God and repentance for sin. Such acts of purification prepare me for the fullest union, a gift that comes in receptive presence to God in the dark night of faith.

To obtain this likeness to God thus demands effort on my part. I have to discipline my life actively by practices like retreat, recollection, spiritual reading. I have to be open to the communication of the Divine in the context of the sacred word. Once I recognize in myself and my culture obstacles to receptive listening, I must try to counterbalance these by establishing in my life, both inwardly and outwardly, attitudes and conditions that aid my growth in likeness to Our Lord.

Since the wonder of the Incarnation, the way to God is Christ, the incarnated Eternal Word. I must be united with Him through grace so that I may share in the divine nature and that Christ may live in me.[36] It is not enough merely to desire this union; I must do something to achieve this likeness. The means are not new. They are ways tried, true, and tested by spiritual masters of many traditions. St. Bernard names them chastity, penance, compunction of heart.

St. John names them detachment, solitude, recollection. I need the advice of these masters not to go astray. As they did, I need to nourish my soul by reading Holy Scripture, the Fathers of the Church, the lives of the saints. These writings bring me back to the roots of faith. They help me achieve the union of likeness by making me a more ready recipient of grace. Deepening myself in this way — by reading what God says of Himself in Holy Scripture and interpretations of His word in the writings of recognized spiritual masters — I may become more Christ-like. There will be a flow back and forth between the presence of Christ within me and my actualizing of this presence in daily life. The soul must seek God, St. Bernard says. This is what life is all about: '... set your hearts on his kingdom, and these others things will be given you as well."[37] It requires sincerity of effort on my part to establish inner and outer conditions for this transformation. The transformation to likeness is itself a gift, but, with God's grace, I can ready myself to receive it.

The Solitary Bird

In these final pages of Part One, I want to explore some conditions for receptivity. Inspired by St. John of the Cross, I shall reflect on the "solitary bird" and what its flight says about becoming a spiritual reader. For the solitary bird is the contemplative soul, transcending mediocrity and seeing into the essence of things. What characterizes its flight is a clue to the proper disposition that must be mine as I approach the spiritual word.

> The characteristics of the solitary bird are five. The first is that it soars as high as it is able. The second, that it can endure no companionship, even of its own kind. The third, that it places its beak against the wind. The fourth, that it has no definite colour. The fifth, that it sings sweetly.[38]

These characteristics describe well the attitude of the true spiritual reader.

Soars as High as It is Able

This phrase means that the contemplative soul soars "above transitory things, paying no more heed than if they were not."[39] As high as he is able seems to say that he attains likeness to God in accordance with the degree of light God Himself gives. For some the light of God in their lives is like a roaring fire; for others it is like a single spark. God dispenses His light as He wills and no one but God knows why some receive more light, others less. However much light I receive, this is what I must act upon. This degree of light accords with my uniqueness. In this sense, every man is potentially a solitary bird, called to soar as high as he is able. But not every man is willing to make this flight because it demands detachment from transitory things in order to be more firmly attached to the Divine, the aim and end of my flight.

The Art and Discipline of Spiritual Reading

Daily I must attempt to detach myself from whatever hinders my flight to God. Only as He gives me the grace to soar above transitory things will this good intent succeed. I must not despair or give up when I find myself falling backward. How imperfect my likeness is. How frustrating not to soar as high as I would like to. I do the best I can with His grace, knowing that I myself cannot set the goal I actually want to reach. That depends on God's plan for my life. All I can do is try at this moment to become more aware of my attachment to transitory things. Perhaps I can pay less heed to them. If He wills it, I can reorder my priorities in light of the goal He is calling me to reach. The rise upward is slow but if I am faithful, His grace will help me to soar higher and higher.

The spiritual reader regards the text as the "launching pad" for this flight. Such words as these, if he reads them openly and humbly, impel his flight to begin. Among the main conditions for launching are attention, consent, and love.

I must discipline my attention to the call of God by going into silence. The flight can only begin if I direct myself to a transcendent horizon. I do so by focusing on the text at hand. I try to diminish the power of distraction on the emotional and functional levels of life. This diminishment of desire enables me to direct my attention to God.

Once I direct my flight to Him, I must consent to His demands on me. My will must more and more become His will for me. This yes must be renewed over and over again; even under the most adverse circumstances, it must be repeated. And unless it comes from the core of my being, my flight cannot begin.

Attention and consent are impossible without love. It is love for God that brings me to the text in the first place. The initiative for this love comes from Him. For no matter how much I love Him and give my life to Him, He has always loved me first. As I tend toward Him, I am tended by Him. He says yes to me long before I say yes to Him. This love that calls me to the Divine strengthens me to endure whatever hardships I may encounter on my flight. Whenever I am about to give up, He gives me the grace to go on. He is a generous God, who keeps after me despite my own fickleness.

> The Lord has ever revealed to mortals the treasures of His wisdom and His spirit; but now that wickedness is revealing her face more and more clearly, He reveals them in large measure.[40]

The eternal now of God's love is there to sustain and carry me at every moment of my flight.

Can Endure No Companionship

The contemplative soul is "so fond of solitude and silence that it can endure the companionship of no other creature."[41] The most solitary of birds is thus

The Art and Discipline of Spiritual Reading

the hermit. He retreats to his shelter to be with God alone and truly wants no other companion. Less solitary than the hermit, though still solitary, is the Christian who follows Christ to the desert or the mountaintop to be alone with the Father. His hermitage is his heart. He guards it jealously even in the midst of the crowd. There is room in his life for a meaningful encounter, but he finds himself less and less absorbed by fleeting contacts with people. Whenever he goes out among men without guarding his heart, he feels that he returns less of a spiritual person. He guards his solitude and is not afraid to be known as a loner sometimes, since to be a Christian is, in comparison to the crowd, to be a solitary bird.

The spiritual reader is aware that the word is addressed to him as *that individual,* as Kierkegaard loved to call himself.[42] The appeal of the word is never to the noisy crowd. Spiritual reading depends on my capacity to be still. I have to discipline my thoughts, feelings, emotions, and perceptions in such a way that my whole inner life slows down and becomes more silent. The busier I am mentally and emotionally, the less chance the word has to illumine my soul.

> How can you expect to keep your powers of hearing when you never want to listen? That God should have time for you, you seem to take as much for granted as that you cannot have time for Him.[43]

The word of God can be heard best in the solitude and silence of my heart. I must first be still and listen; then I can hear if what is calling me is the voice of God or only the seductive ring of a passing fad that takes me further from Him.

Places Its Beak Against the Wind

The contemplative places himself so "as to meet the wind of the Holy Spirit,"[44] that is, he must respond to His inspirations to the end that he may become more worthy of the companionship of Christ. The solitary bird goes against the direction of the wind because only against the wind does the bird attain its full potential for flight.

The contemplative soul has to meet the wind of the Spirit straightforwardly. This means without turning away from the wind no matter how unpleasant its direction might be. For the most part the wind — the inspiration and guidance of the Spirit — comes to me through the ordinary circumstances of daily life. I don't mind facing these situations when they are pleasing and demand little effort. But what about the difficult times, the times of hardship and suffering? I'd like to turn my back on them, but it is exactly in these difficulties that the wind of the Spirit comes. These are the times I am called to detach myself from my yearning for comfort, from my self-centeredness. The storm of adversity is the messenger of the Spirit. It is the uplifting dynamic

The Art and Discipline of Spiritual Reading

that makes me soar above transitory things. That is, it *can be* this dynamic, provided I don't so concentrate on the bad times that I fail to see in them the wind of the Spirit. I might then miss the invitation to soar above my narrow self and find my true self freed in flight for Him. To clear my vision and sharpen my powers of hearing, I need to acquire such a steady habit of turning toward the Divine that even amidst the turmoil of affliction I discover the invitation of the Eternal. Spiritual reading is a powerful means of establishing this inner sensitivity for the Spirit speaking in the events of daily life.

Others may ignore this inner voice; the contemplative soul cannot. He hears the appeal of the Spirit in his inmost self and eagerly responds, places himself against the wind and soars as high as he is able. He comes as close as he can in this life to what God intends him to be. He realizes to the fullest possible degree the presence of God within. He decreases so that Christ may increase. And he is uplifted to these heights of contemplation by the wind of grace, by the inbreathing of the Holy Spirit.

Spiritual reading progresses with infinite patience to uncover and make concrete these patterns of likeness. As the soaring bird gracefully falls and rises, played by the wind and playing with it, so too I let the text take the initiative. Should it speak today, fine; should it remain silent, I'll try again tomorrow. There is no rush. I am not going anywhere but I will sense when I have arrived where the Lord wants me to be. I know that I may misread the word unless I am open to the enlightenment of the Spirit. So before I begin to read, I pray, "Come Holy Spirit, enlighten my heart and enkindle in me the fire of your love." A prayer to the Holy Spirit, prior to reading, helps to place me in the proper receptive mood.

I turn to the text as I would greet an old friend. Even the way I handle it tells me that I am in a different mood, less aggressive, more reflective. Compare what happens when I have a term paper due. Then my powers of mastery come to the fore. I go to the card catalogue, finger the files rapidly, write down a number of references. I rush into the open stacks like a hunter after game, curse when the book I want is out. I go along at a furious pace, picking off the shelves as many references as I can find, lug them over to the desk, check them out, leave the library, load them into my car, zoom off, prepared to study the rest of the afternoon. My approach, perhaps rightly in this case, is not too gentle or loving. Neither is it very playful. My actions express a functional approach to the task of writing a term paper.

It is wise to keep in mind, as I read, the difference between informational and spiritual reading. There is a time and a place for both kinds of reading, but one should not become a substitute for the other. The basic difference between them has to do with the problem-solving style of informational reading and

The Art and Discipline of Spiritual Reading

the dwelling, ruminating, abiding style of spiritual reading.

Reading to gather information is necessarily a linear movement, different from the playful gracious flight of the bird, different from its finding the perfect spot to land and resting there quietly for a while. To ready my term paper, I have to go from point to point, never resting for long in one place. I search right and left for the answers I seek and feel lost if I cannot find a solution to my problem. Until I have the solution I feel tense. I amass more information, determined to survey the field until the right solution is found.

Spiritual reading calls for a different movement, less predatory, more playful. Its pattern is not linear but spiral. I stand in one spot and go deeper, not with the intention to solve a problem but with the patience to read daily whether or not I reach the spiritual light I seek. The fact that nothing may happen is no reason to give up. I must quietly continue reading. Indeed when I do daily spiritual reading weeks and weeks may pass without any light. If I continue waiting upon the word through regular reading in the right attitude, my good will "to do the best I can" is the surest sign of my love for God. Faithful to my daily reading, I await patiently the day He chooses again to give me some light, however far this day may be. I read not to gain something but to show God my good will.

APPROACHING THE SACRED

Like the bird seeks its natural nesting ground, so too when I do spiritual reading I seek to return to my homeland, the place where my roots sink deeply into the truth, doctrine, and mystery of the faith. I am not an explorer of new lands now, as I was when gathering information. I am more like a weather beaten farmer who tills the same soil year after year and never ceases to marvel at its capacity to yield good fruit. The more I dwell on these texts, the more I see emerging from their depths new lights, new appeals, new paths to follow. Paths full of darkness, mystery, and threat, where emptiness and aridity prevail. Blank walls as well as openings through which the light shines forth.

Words of such depth call me home from waywardness and help me dwell in wonder. I return to the place from which I started, only to see it as if for the first time. In this sense spiritual reading is non-utilitarian. It serves no functional purpose as does research for a term paper. Its first meaning is to deepen my presence to God. Its message brings me to rest.

In my stillness with these words I am united with the Divine Word. I try to "taste and savor" the goodness of the Lord. I know in advance that I am incapable of filling myself up. Rather I have to be filled up by the secret communication of the Divine to me. In the overflow of His grace, He uses the

The Art and Discipline of Spiritual Reading

vehicle of the spiritual word to enrich my life. I go from spiritual reading refreshed, but this refreshment is not of my doing.

This refreshed feeling is unlike the "stuffed feeling" I may have at the end of a day of library work. The feeling of being overly full stays with me until I finally get the words and ideas I've collected down on paper. By contrast, in relation to the spiritual word, no amount of rumination, of chewing it over and over again, ever seems to cause that satiated feeling.

When reading for information, I may be "on the take." My goal is to "wring the text dry" of whatever information it has to yield in reference to my topic. In spiritual reading, I recognize myself as a being who is taken up. I am grateful for the gift quality of the spiritual word. Far from being able to wring it dry, I view it as a bottomless well whose living waters never suffer depletion. The text is a keyhole through which I gaze at spiritual horizons I can never hope to cross in one lifetime. Each time I look through the keyhole, I see something I did not see before. The treasure of wisdom in the text is inexhaustible and thus it can't be thrown away. I must return to it again and again.

If I find myself with some leisure time for spiritual reading, I try to resist the temptation to fill it up with other activities. This tendency to fill up time makes it difficult to be a disciplined listener. Spiritual reading is best done in free or leisurely time, in an atmosphere where the ticking of the clock ceases to take over.

When I do informational reading, I am aware that I have only so much time in which to get something read. In spiritual reading clock time should give way to unhurried being with. True, on certain days every minute seems an hour. But, on other days, the time I spend with the text is like the time lovers spend together. A minute is an hour and an hour is a minute. I have a sense of God's good time. The pressure to succeed is off. I have no task to finish, nothing to be accomplished. Five lines or five pages, it doesn't matter as long as I am present to what I read.

I try also to create a special atmosphere when I read, for spiritual reading is not just a matter of running my eye over the page. The room in which I do my reading is a quiet place that has good ventilation and a certain order. I sit there for a while and breathe deeply, trying to quiet my agitated mind. Occasionally I may walk while I'm reading, an alternative style for people who enjoy reading to the leisurely pace of walking in a garden or room. It seems wise not to do my reading immediately after my main meals. I find it best to read either early in the morning or later in the evening when my work is done. I try to make this a set time and go back to the

The Art and Discipline of Spiritual Reading

same place. Such regulation of time, place, and style of reading already begins in me the process of recollection. A "centering down" takes place. By quieting my busy, active mind, by recollecting my dispersed emotions, I create in myself the proper predisposing mood of silence. Inwardly I am still; outwardly I seek stillness. Instead of demanding in advance that the text tell me something I want to hear, I let it speak. Because of my non-violent approach, I leave room for the light of wisdom to enter in.

Even with these preparations, I may still be left in darkness. Spiritual reading is not a kind of magic by which I conjure up presence to the Lord. I cannot force His coming. I can only hold myself in readiness. The discipline of reading helps me to cope with difficulties like spiritual dryness. I go on day after day trusting that God sees my struggles. My success I leave to Him. Such reading shows my desire to listen should He choose the channel of the word to reveal His Holy will.

Has No Definite Color

I am comparing the qualities of the true spiritual reader with the traits of the solitary bird St. John describes. I have seen its soaring and my need to follow the call of God; its aloneness and my need for silence to hear the word; its pattern of flight and my

APPROACHING THE SACRED

need for a spiraling approach. What else does this image of the solitary bird say about the true spiritual reader?

Having "no definite color" in this text of St. John's means that the contemplative must desire to do "no definite thing save that which is the will of God."[4][5] In this image, St. John teaches that I must keep steadfast the desire to do the will of God. The way to attain this union of my human will with the Divine Will is to imitate Our Lord.

Look at Him. He had no definite color. He was always intent upon following His Father's will. Therefore, the divine light could shine through Him unblemished and radiate to the world. This light appealed to the inner man. Outwardly such a man as Peter might appear like others but inwardly he was transformed. God had wrought an irreversible change in him because He chose to follow Christ. His previously manifold desires were reduced to one: to hear the will of God and heed it in whatever way he was called to serve. For the most part this service would go unnoticed. But there would be no standing back if he were called to witness for the faith.

Having no definite color does not take away my likes and dislikes. I retain them. They show up in my evaluations and decisions but do not become the final criteria. When failure, illness, or pain strike me, I certainly suffer but I do not rebel. I see in these

The Art and Discipline of Spiritual Reading

instances the loving will of God that alone is the end of my desire.

Having no definite color does not imply a stale and listless human life, a life that attributes everything to fate and wallows in self-pity. Far from it. This life is a standing forth in courage to undertake the painful process of spiritual transformation. It takes the risk of cutting the thread of earthly security to be totally open to the Spirit. It is a thoughtful life, capable of deciding when self-interest excludes God and when it is time, with His grace, to change course. It is a life that day by day, however thick the darkness, attempts to answer His call, a life that decreases so that He may increase.

Having no definite color does not mean merely retaining an exterior colorlessness, being unnoticed for its own sake. Rather St. John refers to an interior attitude of surrender to God, whether I stand in the center of attention or on the sidelines.

It is likely to happen that the person who forgets himself to such a degree will not attempt to draw attention to himself. The solitary bird prefers the hidden life but this is only a consequence of his inner attitude of desiring to do no definite thing but the will of God. The contemplative soul is content to work along quietly day by day, not calling undue attention to himself, while living in serene presence to Our Lord. He is in the world, but, solitary that he is, not of it. He blends in like the apostle but is unafraid to stand forth when he is called upon to lead. He does not seek the spectacular. He has no need to be noticed but if notoriety comes he bears with it until he can be hidden once again.

The spiritual master affirms the value of hiddenness for the person who wants to imitate Christ. To be hidden in Christ brings the greatest joy. This is the life of the simple. It is the life of everyday. In the hidden growth from acorn to oak, I witness the mystery and fullness of live. The hidden life of nature is quiet and steady. It goes on year after year unnoticed and yet every year, in a hidden way, new growth occurs. A seed is planted and forgotten. And suddenly one day the plant is there. Only in such hiddenness do miracles of growth occur. The same is true for the spiritual life. Christ plants the seed of divine union within my soul. For years this seed may be forgotten. Then one day, imperceptibly yet with determination, it will start to grow.

The catalyst for this growth may have been a spiritual text. Through reading, the hidden life of grace begins its transforming work in the soul. The old man dies; the new man is born. And when did all this happen? It is hard to set the time and place, for such conversion is usually hidden from view. Only occasionally is it sudden, like the conversion of St. Paul. Most of the time all I can say is that it happened. One day there were a few buds and the next thing I knew I was picking a bouquet. Growth is such a quiet thing.

Sings Sweetly

This is the last quality of the solitary bird described by St. John. The contemplative soul "must sing sweetly in the contemplation and love of its Spouse."[46] Freed from earthy attachment, the soul sings sweetly its song of love. The psalmist says that the heavens declare the glory of God not by speaking but simply by being what they are. So too the contemplative's life becomes a song to God. Centered wholly in Our Lord, his life is a song of praise. In a sense, he sings when he serves, when he suffers, when he prays. He sings sweetly because the moving force of his life is love. Harshness and bitterness give way gradually to the kindness and gentility of peace and dedication. Pain and turmoil touch only the periphery of his existence. In the center, in the still point of the soul, his life is a sweet song of love in unison with the divine love song that calls forth the world in sacred harmony.

Whether in poetry or prayer, song or spiritual prose, the man of God is inclined to address the Beloved, to praise His name, to tell of His wondrous ways. This kind of expression is the outward form of the inner life. In such words man speaks of his nearness to God. His language is hallowed. It must be listened to with the utmost respect.

To read these writings, I need to become not just an average reader but an educated reader. This does not mean that I should have a lot of head knowledge. A person can be an exegetical expert and still listen to the text only on the level of technical observer. To be an educated reader, in the etymological sense of the word, I have to allow myself to be "led out" of ego-centered living and "led into" a life centered in my Lord Jesus. I try to see things more with His eyes now. I try to think less of myself so I can be more open to Him.

At times the text leads me to worshipful contemplation of His wonder. At times it leads me to the silence of desert places. Reading in this sense "re-creates" me more in the image God intends me to be; it helps me realize more deeply the divine likeness I am called to become. I can remain indifferent to the truths the text discloses if I so choose. However, to be touched by the truth of the text, even to allow the text to radically change my life, is my first intention as spiritual reader. Should light come, my aim is not to remold the text to suit me but to find myself through the truths it reveals. In this way reading may become an occasion for spiritual growth.

Such an occasion is especially evident in that most profound of reading experiences: the "ah ha" moment. I discover in the words of the spiritual writer an expression of exactly what I have been feeling and would have wanted to say had I found the words to say it. The "ah ha" experience makes me "taste and savor" these words, giving thanks to God for the writer who wrote them and praising Him for allowing me to find a voice for my experience.

Value is no longer a goal I have to seek outside of myself but something I find within. My encounter with the text redeems me from the narrowness of former horizons. Life becomes a field of play not an arena of conquest. While I may not agree with every word of the text, my no is never so final as to exclude the possibility of some kind of yes. My yes and no hover together. Ultimately, for all its seriousness, life is simple if I can see it as a whole — the way God does. In Him all contradictions are finally reconciled.

Conclusion

The spiritual writer sees at moments of utmost clarity the wholeness and oneness all men seek. I may see it too if I dwell thoughtfully on his words. The language of the spiritual writer is a language of liberation. It frees me from such concentration on the parts of life that I forget about the whole. Old in expression, it is rich in content. Unlike the language of technique, that grows obsolete from day to day, it is forever fresh, speaking anew to each generation about the secrets of spiritual growth.

Without disciplining myself to set aside time for meditation, meditative reading, spiritual reading, I cannot hope to discover this deeper life. Taking time to be more reflective is a sign that I want to live not only in man's time but in God's time. I want to utilize my time in such a way that it can become His time. The proper time sense for the spiritual person always involves seeing the eternal piercing the temporal. Within God's time things are eternally present. His will is being done now though I may not be able to see it. Such patience removes the pressure of the moment. What seemed so important is not that earth shaking after all. Let me simply live as best as I can, trusting that He will never fail those who love Him.

Spiritual reading in its fullest sense is a participation in the eternal. It is an act of worship, praise, and thanksgiving. Worship of the Divine for having revealed Himself to me. Praise of Him as He is and not as I would have Him be. "To the One who is sitting on the throne and to the Lamb, be all praise, honor, glory and power, for ever and ever."[4][7] And thanksgiving for allowing to emerge in my midst the words of spiritual masters who become God's messengers and communicate wisdom that might otherwise remain undisclosed. By reading their words and living them in daily life, I do my part to keep alive this sacred dialogue. For if mine is a God Who has spoken to His people, He is also a God Who needs to be heard, if only by a handful of His chosen.

PART TWO

A Personal Reading of the *Cautions* of John of the Cross

The First Reading

It is a cold winter evening. I can hear the wind whistling against the window of my apartment. I sit in a softly lighted room, high atop a hill, overlooking a modern American city. Spread before me for miles and miles are the twinkling lights that signal day's end.

The city is quiet at eventide. A peacefulness settles upon it. Still I am aware of its activity. Skyscrapers alight against a gray skyline project its power. Each day men leave their homes and enter these tall buildings to carry on the business of the world. Days are spent making decisions, writing letters, organizing departments, catering to the public.

In this city too dwell men of prayer. Knowing this gives me hope. People today are tempted to worship the god of technological power. The city is a tribute to this power. It stretches before me, a formidable babel of lights and energy, concrete and construction.

Yet in this same city I meet men of prayer. They know moments of rest. They worship the one true God. Him alone do they adore. I recall the story of one such man that inspires my reflections this evening.

He was successful by city standards, having undergone years of study to become a medical doctor. His practice was affluent; he also taught at a university. Baptized a Catholic, he had married in the Church, but for the most part his was a Sunday only religion. If he missed Mass occasionally, it did not upset him that much. He believed in God; he knew that some ultimate power had to sustain the universe. Then, too, he was a man of science. He witnessed man's capability to conquer diseases that in the past meant certain death. He believed in science. He felt secure when surrounded by test tubes, microscopes, and x-ray apparatus. In short, he was a man of the city, a man of science, and not really a man of prayer.

Then something happened. One day he discovered that he had been married for twenty-five years. He had been blessed with a lucrative profession and a good family life, but he had never said thanks for all of this. He wanted to do something to express his gratitude. Much against the advice of friends and colleagues, but with the support of wife and sons, he decided to volunteer for six months service in a war zone overseas. He began working in one of the hospitals, inconspicuously, compared to the recognition he received at home.

A Personal Reading of the Cautions of John of the Cross

One unforgettable day, as he relates the story, an event occurred that subsequently changed his life. He could not explain how but he felt standing beside him, working with him, the person of Christ. This was no experience whose validity he could prove. He simply knew that Christ was there, blessing the work he had volunteered to do. This sense of Christ's presence came to him as a gift he was unworthy to receive. Try as he might, he could not deny the feeling that Christ was beside him, helping in some mysterious way to fulfill his destiny.

The man returned home, changed now because Christ was his constant companion. Mass was no longer a once-a-week duty but a daily sacrifice he attended with joy. He felt the loss of those many years in which he had failed to deepen his presence to the Lord. There were many roads to the spiritual life as yet unexplored by him, and he hastened to seek the advice of a spiritual director. He also began reading classic spiritual writers — Thomas à Kempis and Teresa of Avila, Francis de Sales and John of the Cross. In their words he found the wisdom he was seeking. They understood his experience and affirmed the transformation he had undergone. Christ was for them too the center of life. In these writers he found companions who shared his spiritual quest and could help him discover how best to serve the Lord.

Many miles distant from this man's home lives a woman who also found Christ at the core of her existence. She is an inspiration to those who know her, for her capacity to endure suffering is great. Yet she is the first to admit that pain is overcome by the consolation she receives in prayer. No day passes without at least one hour of meditation. No day goes by without a renewed awareness that this imperfect world is made liveable and loveable by Christ's presence. And each day she tries to do something, no matter how small, to express her gratitude.

I think of these two this evening as I read and reflect upon a few passages from the *Cautions* of John of the Cross.[1] For many years St. John has been the best loved writer of this woman. He reminds her that if all things are lived in Christ's name no burden is too great to bear. Sanctity is inseparable from one's capacity to endure suffering in Christ's name.

St. John directs these cautions to Carmelite sisters, but they are valuable for every Christian. Anyone who is truly religiously minded, that is, anyone who would choose to live a deeper spiritual life, can benefit from reading them.

I pause right away on the word "caution." Slowness, patience, caution are among the most frequently repeated words of the spiritual master. The Spirit is in no hurry. His ways are ways of peace and calm. With this one word, St. John says a wealth of things. I am not to attack the spiritual life as I might dig into the solution of a problem. The ways of the Spirit are not the ways of the world. Sacred time is different from clock time. An hour of meditative reading means

A Personal Reading of the Cautions of John of the Cross

more to me *as me* than many days of unreflective work.

St. John cautions me as I begin my hour of reading to move slowly. Go according to God's time. All good things happen in God's good time. As a clock-bound city dweller, I may find this relaxed position difficult to take. But at least during this pause for spiritual reading, I have to shed my clock-watching tendencies. I have to drop my anxiety to get things done. Move slowly, move gradually, move according to God's own good time and, paradoxically, you may "quickly come to great perfection."[2]

I begin reading. Each word is rich with possibilities for meditative reflection.

> The religious who desires to attain quickly to holy recollection, silence, spiritual detachment and poverty of spirit, wherein is enjoyed the peaceful refreshment of the Holy Spirit and whereby the soul attains to union with God, and frees itself from the hindrances which come from the creatures of this world, and defends itself from the wiles and deceits of the devil, and is disencumbered of itself must needs practice the following instructions.[3]

I look away from the page. There is so much here to dwell upon already before reading what these instructions might be. St. John says what I am seeking through such spiritual exercises as recollection, silence, detachment, and poverty of spirit is "the peaceful refreshment of the Holy Spirit." This expression, "peaceful refreshment," is a beautiful one. I savor its taste and meaning. I ask myself what it is like to feel refreshed in a human way and then try to reflect upon how much more refreshing must be the gift of the Spirit.

Remember a hot July day. You are working in the garden. You trim the dead leaves at the base of each tomato plant. It is time also to tie the bean shoots to poles. You have forgotten the string, so you return to the workshed for the cord you thought was in your pocket. The number of bean plants seems infinite, but you tie them all. That job done, you decide to hoe the dirt around the corn. The earth is hard, sun-parched, so it takes more effort on your part to dig. Your shirt is soaked with sweat. The beads are running down your back. You wipe off the perspiration and go on scraping and turning the earth. Though the garden is a lot of work, it's worthwhile. Everyone enjoys fresh beans and tomatoes. You continue working, trying not to think about how tired and thirsty you are. Footsteps. You turn and see your neighbor standing there. She's carrying a big pitcher of cool lemonade and a frosty glass. You greet her, walk to the edge of the garden, take the glass and drink, slowly at first but then with bigger gulps. You savor the last few mouthfuls, say thanks, and turn to finish off the last two rows, greatly refreshed. Such is the refreshment of the body.

A Personal Reading of the Cautions of John of the Cross

For months now you have been studying for final exams. Books, note cards, cross references are piled high around your room. You feel exhausted. Your mind feels stuffed, unable to absorb any more ideas. You long for a breath of fresh air. Get up from your study table. Go out for a walk. The river is not far away from where you live. You head there. There is something about being near water that clears the mind. You walk briskly to the river's edge and sit down. At first your mind won't stay still. You keep trying to link one idea to the next. But you wait and watch the water. The sun is warm. Coal barges are floating by. A boy is fishing with his dad. A twig drifts into view. You follow it until it is out of sight. Your mind is slowing down. You sit and watch and feel warmed by the sun. Such is the refreshment of the mind.

And what about "the peaceful refreshment of the Holy Spirit"? In some way it must be related to the refreshment of body and mind — similar but not the same. For this is a peace the world cannot give. This is a peace I cannot bring upon myself. The peaceful refreshment of the Spirit comes to me as gift. I cannot demand it willfully; I can only ready myself to receive this gift by recollection, silence, detachment, and poverty of spirit.

In this spiritual refreshment, the soul attains the restfulness it seeks, however many obstacles block its path. Uncountable are the wiles and deceits of my false self. Yet the questing soul goes on to pursue its goal of oneness with God. It desires to attain this goal "quickly." If it is willing to follow the path St. John proposes of recollection, silence, detachment, and inner poverty, then union with God shall be the soul's reward.

To reach at oneness with Him, I must free myself from the deceptive ties that bind me to the world. I free myself *from* attachment to things to free myself *for* deeper attachment to God. Detachment is not a negative act. It is a way of distancing myself from the temporal world to bind myself more intimately to the eternal that shines forth in it.

I am to free myself not only from the hindrances of the world and the deceit of the demonic; I must also be "disencumbered" of my self.

Once as a child I took some expensive perfume from my aunt's dresser, thinking it would never be missed. I was wrong. Since I had used what I took, playing "make-believe," it was too late to make restitution and I was too embarrassed to confess. For many days I was weighed down by a feeling of guilt. I asked myself again and again, "How could you do it?" I had never done anything like that before. All my questioning served only to increase the burden that weighed me down. At last I decided to confess. I had to admit the wrong I had done and ask forgiveness. I went to my aunt and told her that it was I who had taken the perfume she was looking for

A Personal Reading of the Cautions of John of the Cross

last week. To my surprise she had forgotten the incident and thanked me because I trusted her enough to confess. Of course, she forgave me. My guilt was lifted and I felt lighthearted at last.

This was for me an experience of being "disencumbered" of some part of myself that had become foreign to me, namely, my guilt at having taken something that did not belong to me. Is there something in this experience that can help me to understand what St. John means by being disencumbered of my self?

One dimension of self that hinders spiritual growth is the side of me that wants to manage the world, my seemingly self-sufficient ego. Making this ego ultimate is one obstacle I must disencumber myself from, if I am ever to experience the peaceful refreshment of the spiritual life. Such refreshment comes to me only when I die to my old self and find new life in the Divine.

The process of disencumbering myself from my ego as ultimate is long and arduous. St. John says he will instruct me. Here is the first step.

> With habitual care and with no further labour or other kind of exercise, failing not of his own part to do that which his state enjoins on him, he will very quickly come to great perfection, gaining all the virtues together and attaining to holy peace.[4]

What are the conditions St. John proposes if I want

to profit from his instructions? The phrase that first holds my attention is "habitual care," like the care a good mother shows her children. Her concern is habitual. Without attracting undue attention to herself, she cooks breakfast, washes clothes, decorates their rooms. She listens to hassles over friends and teachers before tucking them in, leads their prayers, and kisses them good-night. Hers is an habitual care; it's second nature to her. She doesn't think about it; she simply cares.

When I apply this caution to my own life, St. John seems to say do well what you have to do. Perfection is not an impossible dream. Live daily life with its duties and responsibilities, its ups and downs, but do so with habitual care. Within the common life of everyday routine resides the road to holiness, if I live my life in the proper way. I need to stand by my commitments. I must be faithful to the values of Christian life I witness to. And I must try to grow in humility and respect. Through prayer, meditation, and spiritual reading, the ways of the Lord should become second nature to me — so habitual that every action is an expression of my love for Him. I imitate the Lord with such habitual care that selfishness lessens its power over me.

St. John says, moreover, that the everyday life should be led "with no further labour or other kind of exercise." What does the phrase "no further labour" imply? Perhaps St. John is saying that I ought not to make any *extra*-ordinary efforts to live the life of holiness. For then I might concentrate more on myself and my progress than on God. Rather I must strive to live spiritually within the routine day to day existence that is mine. The danger of attempting to seek the Spirit by extraordinary means may lead to making these means ends in themselves.

In ordinary things like cooking a meal and caring for children, Jesus can be found. Further labor to find His Spirit is often not necessary, for He resides at the center of the life I am called to live now. If I am a sister, to do my work for Him and utilize the time celibacy offers me for frequent recollection and retreat. If I am a mother, to care for husband and children out of love for God in such a way that I make it easier for them to find God in daily life. If I am a career woman, to guard against becoming so bound to professional status that I neglect my need for prayer.

By simply remaining open to God's presence in and behind every ordinary appearance, I will "quickly come to great perfection." This perfection is not that of a perfectly balanced equation; it is the perfection of paradox.

Paradox is something apparently contrary to logical conclusion but nonetheless experientially true. The Christian message is couched in paradox. Do good to those who hate you. Pray for those who hurt you. Give to him who takes from you. The proof of such paradoxical statements is found not in the telling of them but in the living. For the faithless man suffering and sorrow breed despair; for the spiritual man affliction is counted a blessing. Sickness of body brings true sight to the soul. Emptiness is the necessary condition for being made full. Unknowing is the truest knowing. Feeling the absence of God, I may be implicitly aware of His real presence. Whereas the life of the ego tempts me to be everything, the life of the spirit asks only that I will one thing. The ego says find yourself; the spirit says forget yourself. In the eyes of the world, you can be a failure; in the eyes of God a man of great spiritual good.

In many of his writings, St. John follows the way of paradox.[5] To find pleasure in everything, desire pleasure in nothing. To possess everything, desire to possess nothing. To be everything, desire to be nothing.

If God is to be my all, then anything less than God must be annihilated as a last concern. Man as ego and body lives the life of desire. No sooner is one wish fulfilled than another presents itself. Desire is never satisfied. Thus a first step to spiritual living is the banishment of uncontrolled desire that breeds agitation, restlessness, lack of inner peace. The fruits of the spirit are liberation, tranquillity, restfulness in God.

To attain to the deeper meaning of everything, possession of all, the fullness of life, I must find

A Personal Reading of the Cautions of John of the Cross

nothing less than God himself in all things. To gain all the virtues together, to be blessed with holy peace, I must cling faithfully to the imitation of Christ. "To this end," St. John goes on to say, "it must first be noted that the evils which the soul receives come from the enemies aforementioned — namely, the world, the devil and the flesh."[6]

"The world is the least difficult enemy." Perhaps this is so for the cloistered sister but is it the same for me? Not exactly. For me and you, who live in the world, the struggle just to keep ahead economically is often great — with children to educate and mortgages to pay. Life in the world is not that simple. No matter how much I want to practice detachment, the harsh demands of daily necessities often catch me unaware. Before I know it, I am caught in the struggle for power and possession. Still what St. John says makes good sense if I want to steady myself on the right path once again. His words help me see my life in proper perspective.

When I reflect upon the essential temporality of my existence, the world at that moment ceases to be a great enemy. I am no longer bound to a spirit of materialism. I can love the world and use well its gifts, knowing at the same time that material goods cannot ultimately satisfy me. Everything that promises fulfillment passes away. Only one thing does not pass away, the spirit of Our Lord. He tells us that His kingdom is not of this world. We who follow Him must be in this world but not of it. We must learn that it is in Him that we find peace.

> I have told you all this
> so that you may find peace in me.
> In the world you will have trouble,
> but be brave:
> I have conquered the world.[7]

The world holds no lasting fascination when it is wholly informed by Christ. Christ himself shows us the secret of overcoming this world when he goes into the desert for forty days. He is tempted there by all the world has to offer — power, pleasure, possession — if only He will betray His trust in the Father. The devil is sent hastily away, for the Lord knows that his promises are lies.

"The devil," St. John says, "is the hardest to understand." The difficulty seems related to the general inability on man's part to comprehend the mystery of iniquity. Why is there so much suffering in the world? Is there no resolution to the inner torment described by St. Paul?

> The fact is, I know of nothing good living in me — living, that is, in my unspiritual self — for though the will to do what is good is in me, the performance is not, with the result that instead of doing the good things I want to do, I carry out the sinful things I do not want.[8]

Is the power of evil always there to pervert the good?

A Personal Reading of the Cautions of John of the Cross

Such questions are not easy to answer.[9] For the moment I can only repeat what St. John says. The prince of darkness, the power of evil, is the enemy hardest to understand.

A related reason for this difficulty seems to be that the demonic is present under so many disguises. Evil is difficult to discern. False gods may be erected before we recognize them. In our age, technology may become the only god we obey. Outwardly the quest for power may triumph over human concern. Inwardly the demonic may take the form of envy, jealousy, deceit.

And what of the flesh? St. John says it "is the most tenacious of all and its assaults continue for so long as the old man exists." The old man is he who has heard the word but failed to heed it. He is a victim of the flesh not merely in the sexual sense but of flesh in its other forms, such as pride, anger, agitation, gluttony, and greed. These passions tear his flesh apart. Peace is impossible. The old man manipulates his fellow men. He lies and cheats while playing the pious professional. He clings to his wealth as if coffers piled high will guarantee him a place in heaven.

When Christ came, he held up a mirror to man. In that mirror man saw his old self. He did not like what he saw and so declared himself a sinner. He would repent before the Lord who came to redeem him. In this way he would put off his old self and become a new man. He used to hate his enemies; now Christ preached forgiveness. Once he strove for glory; now he would be meek. Baptized in Christ's name, he felt a sense of rebirth.

> In a short time the world will no longer see me;
> but you will see me,
> because I live and you will live.
> On that day
> you will understand that I am in my Father
> and you in me and I in you.[10]

To be baptized in Christ does not mean that I will cease sinning. Pride is not easily overcome; neither is my propensity for deception. I have been given new life by God's grace. He found me worthy to redeem. Now I must become more Christ-like everyday, though this struggle may meet with only limited success.[11] The old man clings tenaciously to me. I must repent again and again, but as long as I am trying Christ will give me strength. No effort of my own can ever totally transform me. Only the gift of His grace can make me wholly new. Nonetheless through this grace, I can ready myself for His presence when it comes to me as gift.

One way of preparing the way is to read Holy Scripture and the writings of the spiritual master. The truths he records about transformation in Christ are validated by experience. The way he outlines is inescapable if I want to put off the old man and put

A Personal Reading of the Cautions of John of the Cross

on the new, leave rational intelligence behind and leap ahead into the darkness of faith.

Closing Prayer

I am going to stop reading, Lord, but I want to tell You how grateful I am. Your goodness overwhelms me. Your graciousness fills me with joy. I know my understanding of these words is terribly limited, yet I want to meditate on them, for I believe they are the words of eternal life. I hope that reading them will help me to say, "Your will be done," and really mean it. Though some event may seem the cause of much unhappiness, I want to have the faith to say that it is good. Let me listen to the words of Your saint so I may find the way in my own life to embody Your eternal, infinite love for souls.

The Second Reading

Subzero temperatures have given way at last to a warm mass of air pushing its way east. Spring is almost here. The chair on which I sit faces outward. I can see the city lights below. People are homeward bound, looking forward to an evening with family and friends. Perhaps after supper some of them will retire to a quiet room for a few moments of recollection. Evening is a good time to gather together the thoughts of the day. It's a good time to read and reflect on the writings of the spiritual master, to listen to what goes on between me and the text.

Something happened this weekend that made concrete the problem of listening.

... You could feel the expectation of the audience as he entered the large and crowded auditorium. High-pitched voices resounded in every corner of the room as the sisters waited for the speaker to begin. He sensed the eager anticipation in the eyes of his audience. He too was part of the troubled times that had brought them here.

Almost as if an invisible curtain had been raised, the audience began to silence itself. The more vociferous groups gave way last, but they too caught the hint that it was time for the speaker to begin. The sister who was introducing him stood at the podium and was greeted with the usual patter of applause.

While she was speaking, many thoughts ran through his mind: "Dear sisters," he said to himself, "you are living in an age when people for the most part deny the relevance of your lives. You are asked to bear much suffering in this time of transition in the Church. May God be with you."

The introduction was drawing to a close. It was as if sister were introducing a stranger, someone he hardly knew, who had been invited to speak to these sisters about the spiritual life when he himself was always and forever on the way.

A Personal Reading of the Cautions of John of the Cross

A burst of applause. It was time for him to speak. He rose and walked to the podium, all the while uttering a short prayer, "Make me an instrument of Your will."

Two sisters sat in the audience. They were on opposite sides of the room. Each prepared to listen to the words the speaker was about to impart.

The one on the left side had told herself the night before that with all her heart she wanted to be open to what he had to say. She might not be able to agree with every point, but she knew that this man was a holy person. He lived with God and could show others the way. True, they might differ in regard to external changes where renewal was concerned; but on this they would be in accord: it had to begin in the spiritual dimension. Committees, questionnaires, experimental groups were only one side of renewal. The other, more basic side, had to do with her personal relationship to God.

Lately she had felt herself slipping. She no longer prayed the way she used to. Now that she could make up her own meditative schedule, she realized that her inner resources were weak. She had little religious experience to fall back upon, and the old formulas did not work any more. She needed to listen to someone who lived with God and could show her the right path. She sat quietly, eyes turned toward the speaker, and prayed, "Let me be open to receive the message he has to give."

The sister on the right side of the auditorium was hardly able to tear herself away from the conversation she was having with some of her friends. They had so many great ideas. They had read so many new books. Next to them, she felt she knew nothing about the latest trends in theology. She had tried to keep abreast of things by taking a course last summer; now it looked as if she would have to enroll again. Either that or take a course in counseling. The sister beside her was enrolled in what sounded like a good program. She had such deep insight into people. Soon she would be setting up encounter groups for her community. It was just this kind of exciting experience that the sisters in her own community were missing. At least this conference would serve one purpose: it would bring her up to date with a lot of new and stimulating ideas she could try to incorporate in her community. Such ideas were bound to aid the sisters in their efforts for renewal.

She tried to calm the inner excitement the conversation had engendered but with little luck. To listen to one speaker for an hour when all around her were so many other interesting speakers seemed a waste of time. They should have broken up into small groups after a fifteen minute introduction. How unpleasant to miss the chance of finding what the others sisters were doing. Oh well, there would be plenty of time for that. One hour more or less did not make that much difference.

A Personal Reading of the Cautions of John of the Cross

She tried again to turn her attention to the speaker. Maybe he would have some good things to say about those theological trends or perhaps he would reconfirm the important contributions of counseling for community renewal programs. It was clear to everybody, she thought, that he did not make a very impressive appearance. So quiet and subdued! He did not seem at all alight with the excitement she felt. How could he be so out of it?

Deep down she really did not think he would have that much to say. One of the sisters who had impressed her most said that in her opinion the speaker had not been well chosen. His ideas were old-fashioned. He seemed to be running away from the risk of renewal. He did not even question the authority of the Church as other avant-garde writers were doing. These writers, she had said, were mature and balanced people, capable of evaluating their own feelings and no longer in need of the structures of the past.

After this conversation, sister did not expect much from the speaker. He would probably make the same old remarks. She read the program once again to assure herself that he was only supposed to speak for fifty minutes. Then it would be time for the group sessions. She yawned once and turned toward him.

The speaker looked out at the faces gazing upward. In some eyes he sensed gentle affirmation, in others hostility. All of these eyes, gentle and angry, belonged to the children of God. With their limited insight, they were trying to serve Him in today's world. All he could do was share with them the insights granted to him by God's grace in his years of meditation and study. Whether he would succeed or fail in bringing his message to them was of no real concern.

His words were simple and not really new but they emerged from his heart. One sister beheld him as a spiritual master to whom she could listen with confidence. One sister saw only a tired old man whose notions were obsolete. With one he succeeded; with one he failed, though these fruits of his effort remained unknown to him.

This experience says something to me as I read St. John. I am aware that certain problems emerge when reading a spiritual master out of the past. Like these sisters, I can only listen to this master through the filter of my own experience. Temperamentally and by disposition, I am bound to color what I read.

It is especially difficult today to read a past spiritual master because I have lost the real sense of spiritual reading. Instead of opening myself in obedience to his words, I am likely to try to force him to fit into my mold. Instead of listening quietly, I find myself on the defensive. He says solitude; I say encounter. He stresses silence; I snap back with the danger of isolation. He advises obedience; I defend our new found freedom. He recalls me to recollec-

A Personal Reading of the Cautions of John of the Cross

tion; I opt for more activity. How else can we serve God's poor?

I want this spiritual master to conform to me instead of disposing myself to him. I want to lead the spiritual master instead of being led. I judge his words obsolete before even hearing them as a whole. In my arrogance I reverse the master-disciple relationship. Disciple becomes master; master is relegated to the role of disciple.

This reversal of a fundamental spiritual relationship can only lead to disastrous results. How can an initiate possibly know more than a man experienced in this way of life? How can a disciple teach his master?

The master-disciple relationship needs to be reinstated when I do spiritual reading. I must be open and obedient to the words of the master, even if I do not understand all that this obedience implies. I simply trust that somehow God has chosen this person as a channel by which to reveal Himself to me. The master may say things that upon later reflection seem contrary to my style of life, but at the moment of listening my place is not to judge the master but to abide by his word. In saying yes, I ready myself should God choose to enter my life by way of the spiritual word. He will find waiting for him a person of humble openness, not an arrogant judge.

A disciple may refuse to obey his master on the

grounds that he must remain open to everyone. In reality he is open to no one but himself. If he can convince himself that truth is relative, that one piece of advice is as good as another, he can indulge all his desires. He never has to settle down. He tastes every new dish that comes along. Nausea may be the high price he will have to pay for his uncommitted life.

Spiritual reading thus implies disposing myself in an obedient way to the wisdom of the writer. His words have met the test of time and will not pass away because of my prejudiced view. Let me listen rather than lose another opportunity for spiritual deepening.

When I turn to St. John, then, my wish is not to change him but to be changed by him. I want him to know that my path to God is overrun by many obstacles, that I no longer know the way. I have read a lot of books. I have talked with colleagues and friends. But this is not enough. I need to stand before him, ready to the best of my ability to obey his words. I want to dispose myself in such a way that they may touch my heart.

When St. John speaks, his words are clear and to the point. He says, "In order to conquer any one of these three enemies, [the world, the devil, and the flesh] it is necessary to conquer them all three; and if one is weakened, the other two are weakened: and, when all three are conquered, no more war remains in the soul."[12]

A Personal Reading of the Cautions of John of the Cross

Immediately these words remind me of the war that exists in my own soul. I have been restless of late. These three great powers separate me from the Sacred so I must reflect on each one in turn. I remember what St. Augustine said, that my heart would be restless until it rests in You. These enemies keep me restless. But to weaken one is to weaken all and, "when all three are conquered, no more war remains in the soul."

Enemy Number One: The World

The world is too much with me. Morning dawns. Light banishes my night time reverie. The world rushes in upon me. Is my first thought to ask Him to bless this day? Hardly. I flick on the radio for the weather report. The war. A local fire. The five-day forecast. And the world rushes in upon me. I feel thirsty. I feel hungry. Is my first thought to thank Him for a refrigerator full of food? Not really. I pull open the door, down some juice, make toast and coffee, while the world rushes in upon me. My day. In my mind I schedule the appointments that will occupy the morning hours. No time for a leisurely lunch. Rush. There is a rescheduled committee meeting I must attend. I have an hour or so to prepare my report. Rush. I should have typed it the night before. I have to be subtle, diplomatic when it's my turn to present. Hurry now. I finish dressing, slam the front door, run down the steps, jump into the car, turn on the ignition. Nothing. The engine won't start. Be calm. It's cold. Turn on the key again. Ignition. I'm off. The stop light is turning yellow. Why wait for the red? I gun the engine. Made it! I drive on, down the hillside, across the bridge. Minor traffic jam. I move into the other lane and give the car some gas. Up one hill, up the next. Good. My favorite parking place is free. I swing in and shut off the motor. Out of the car, up the steps, into the elevator. Find my office keys, unlock the door, hang up my coat, look at the clock. Just on time!

In all these ways, I make the world my enemy. In its "worldliness" it rushes in upon me and fills every minute of my life with worldly concerns. I forget that with each tick of the clock I am that much closer to eternity. My attitude has to change. The world only becomes my enemy when I allow it to alienate me from my Source. Then the temporal makes me unmindful of the eternal.

I am beginning to understand St. John's caution against the world. The world in itself is not my enemy. I make it my enemy when my attitude toward it isolates me from the eternal. Cautioned by St. John I may catch myself before it is too late. Then my day will be the same, but there will be a noticeable change in my attitude toward it.

Morning dawns. I awaken slowly and take an extra moment to say thanks for the gift of this day. I eat and feel grateful for the food on my table. While

A Personal Reading of the Cautions of John of the Cross

dressing, I try to center my thoughts on the Lord. "Even if I do not think of You explicitly, let me do what I do for Your sake." While watching my driving, I can still take a few moments for recollection. I stop at the traffic light and look out over hills, knowing that His presence is everywhere. I intersperse mental plans for my morning with brief meditations on His providential care. In this way I save myself a lot of needless aggravation over a day that will work itself out anyway. By the time I arrive at the office, my working day has already taken on a deeper meaning. What might have been a merely functional approach is replaced by a rhythmic blend of action and contemplation, labor and leisure — and all because of a shift in attitude. Whether preparing reports or chairing meetings, my whole approach will be more calm and peaceful, if my time is grounded in the eternal. I realize that I can be patient. Life is a gradual unfolding. What I do not accomplish today, I can do tomorrow. My time becomes more God's time. In his good time, all tensions are resolved.

In this way, the world, instead of being my enemy, becomes my friend. Instead of keeping me a prisoner from God, it becomes a path that leads me closer to Him.

Enemy Number Two: The Devil

To make me forget my dependence on God is the devil's desire. He plays on my pride and tempts me to think that I can be my own savior. He uses his wiles to make me believe that nothing can stand in the way of my will.

Let's say I have just completed my degree in social work. I am understandably proud, both of the many courses I have taken and of the good grades I have received. I leave the sure surroundings of school mates and faculty and set out to serve my fellow men. My first assignment takes me to a ghetto section of the city. I am armed with much knowledge from books but little from life. Suddenly life confronts me. How can people treat one another so meanly? They lie, cheat, steal. Race against race, for what reason? I want to bring love into this world. I try all of the techniques that worked so well in group sessions at school. They fail to work here. Those that I thought would be most receptive are simply taking advantage of me. They are playing on my good will while looking out for their gain. It is true I reach a few of the people. They understand the love in my heart, but so many others turn away. Is it because I am trying too hard? Such self-examination is painful, so I close it off. I recall instead how proud I am of my education. I must show these people evidence of my good will. I am determined to redeem them from their lack of understanding. Someone has to save them from themselves. I will show them how to overcome hatred and hypocrisy. I will teach them to trust.

A Personal Reading of the Cautions of John of the Cross

The good will I have is thus tainted by willfulness. It is only after I have failed again and again that I may begin to see that it is not these people who are my enemies. My worst enemy is myself. Once I realize how twisted my motives have become, I may be able to avoid the same "devilish" snare in the future. Such an experience may evoke in me a renewed sense of dependence on God — the one sure way to weaken demonic pride. As I begin to delve into my motives, I may see when violence masquerades as love; when pride that I am better than you poses as pity; when the desire for praise hides under the cover of compassion. Admitting failure is not easy, but this admission marks a beginning: the acknowledgment of my sinfulness before God and my need for redemption.

Enemy Number Three: The Flesh

The enmity typical of the flesh is often more subtle than lust. I am equally upset by anger, envy, jealousy, by hostility, anxiety, depression. Anger, for example, is a "fleshy" phenomenon. Its effects can stay with me long after the initial cause has disappeared.

I may be the eldest of two sisters. Around the age of fifteen, I begin to notice more and more what I had tried not to see before: my parents seem to favor my younger sister. Several instances convince me that this favoritism is not a matter of my imagination. It is true that she is brighter than I, more talented in some areas, and quite pretty. When both of us bring good grades home, everyone fusses over her. I am angry at my parents, but I try not to show it. When I do express my feelings, they pay even more attention to her! So I seethe in silence.

The years go by and my sister and I drift apart. Both of us have successful lives. There is nothing to be angry or envious about any more, especially since our parents have died, and I have long since made my peace with them. Nonetheless, something prevents us from becoming close. When my sister is around, I feel the old anger welling up. Not just emotionally but bodily. I realize that I have never really forgiven her, and I have headaches to prove it. I sense that she knows what's wrong, but neither of us wants to make the first move. Anger is tenacious when it remains all cooped up inside. About the only way for us to let bygones be bygones would be for us to talk about it. I resolve to wait for the right occasion and clear the whole thing up.

My resolution is more likely to be carried out if I become aware that my worthwhileness does not depend on my relationship with my parents or my sister; it depends on my relationship with God. With His grace, perhaps I can grow to a deeper level of self-respect from which will emerge a deeper respect for others. In this way my anger toward my sister would be weakened and I can learn to love her as she

A Personal Reading of the Cautions of John of the Cross

truly is instead of clinging to my memories of our mutual past.

Just as the world and the devil may isolate me from God, so too the flesh in this form of anger and hostility separates me from His mercy and love. But if I can weaken one of these enemies, all three will be weakened and I shall be on the way to that peace Christ has promised. Even when these three enemies are not wholly overcome, peaceful refreshment of the Spirit begins to be mine. If the inner struggle does not cease, it at least makes me mindful of my weakness and need for redemption. While some struggle may remain, it gives me an occasion to strive for oneness with God.

Closing Prayer

O Lord, allow the words of this master to touch my heart. When I dwell upon them, let me realize the sinfulness that separates me from Your presence. I can reflect on my three "enemies." I can propose ways of overcoming them. Still in my weakness I am bound to them. From this sphere of failure, I come to You for help. Sinful as I am, I know that I can kneel before You and find awaiting me Your love. This gift of love is freely given and it must be as freely received by me. Such receptivity requires faith — a faith in that which is beyond anything this world can give, a faith in darkness. Grant me the grace I need to live this life of faith. Let me experience each day the struggle to find You and once in a while the joy of being found by You. Grant that my way may become more and more Your way for me. In spite of my unworthiness, I may then become a true disciple of Your word as spoken in the words of the spiritual master. Your word lives among us still in these sacred words. When I read these words, may I be filled with the same spirit the apostles experienced when You looked at them and said, "Follow me."

The Third Reading

About twenty people were gathered in a small classroom. They represented different races, colors, creeds; yet they had all come together for the same purpose: to learn from Eastern wisdom some basic modes of living in the world in a more meditative way. They had spent some weeks conditioning their bodies physically by exercise and fast and were now ready, under the watchful guidance of their teacher, to begin meditation.

The person who would lead them was by no means a spiritual master in the strict sense. She only wished to help them begin the meditative life by becoming aware, physically and emotionally, of ways of using space and time that could bring them closer to their spiritual center. Under her guidance, the group began its usual period of "active relaxation."

A Personal Reading of the Cautions of John of the Cross

"Feel how tense your facial muscles are. Tense them even more. Hold the tension for a moment and then release it slowly. Notice the difference between tension and relaxation. Now tense the muscles in your arms . . . and so on until your entire body feels relaxed. All the while breathe slowly and deeply.

"What we are going to explore this evening is one means of preparing yourself for meditation and that is the taking of a kind of 'visual trip.' It will not take long. At most ten or fifteen minutes. During this trip you will try to come closer to your spiritual center — there where you are at one with all things."

She began speaking softly. The room was silent. Each person was resting within his own mind, within his own body.

"Think of yourself at the foothills of a mountain range. You are going to begin climbing. You will climb until you can go no farther. You will know when you have finished climbing because you will become aware of having found something for which you have been searching for a long time. Let's call it your 'self-symbol.' It is a symbol you can take with you wherever you go. You can always turn to it and it will be there inside you."

Led by the voice of the teacher, each member of the group began to climb. One person later described her journey this way: "It was dark, it was steep, it was rugged going at first. Then I became aware of a soft red glowing light. The light became more intense as I climbed. It was the light I had been searching for. I wanted this light to be my self-symbol."

"When you have found your symbol," the teacher's voice went on, "you can begin to go down the mountain, slowly down the mountain. At its base you will see spread before you endlessly, to infinity, a field of your favorite flowers. Whether you turn to the front or to the back, to the right or to the left, everywhere there are flowers and their fragrance fills the air. Walk into the field of flowers. Sense their softness as they brush across your bare feet. Their fragrance is beautiful. Bend down gently and pick one of your favorite flowers. Hold it in your hands. Admire its delicate beauty. Let its fragrance envelop you. Let yourself move closer and closer into the depths of the flower. Be held by the flower. Let each soft petal gently support you. Now you are one with the flower. Your body feels light, almost weightless. No more busy thoughts clutter your mind. You are like the flower, light and still and whole. You experience the beauty and goodness of the whole. The peace and silence of flower and field. You are silent now, your mind is at rest. Rest now and be one with the flower, be at one with every thing."

Twenty people held the silence for a few moments and those moments were profound. The silence held a bit longer and then someone coughed, another yawned. The journey inward was over for a while. Twenty busy people had entered this room. Twenty

A Personal Reading of the Cautions of John of the Cross

were leaving to resume their various tasks in the world, but they were leaving more quiet, more peaceful than when they had first come in. Most felt less nervous and agitated. They were tired physically but with the good feeling of tiredness that comes after exercise.

A few people spoke of what they saw on the mountaintop. One saw light and wanted this as her self-symbol; another saw a garden, symbol of spring. There was one who saw violence and bloodshed, a plane crash in which there were no survivors, no one but him on the top of the mountain looking at the wreck.

Slowly the classroom emptied and people walked away. Two of them paused to speak together: the one who had seen the light and the other who had seen the violent crash of a plane. This person began to describe the kind of life he was leading. In St. John's way of putting it, he was "possessed by the world." He had gone from common laborer to executive and owner of his own business. He was married, had five lovely daughters and was making more money than he ever dreamed possible when he was just a railroad man. Lately he had begun to ask himself what was the meaning of it all.

"I have so much," he said. "A beautiful home and my kids are in good schools. I have two cars in the garage. My wife and I can take off and travel when we want. I have plenty of money put away for retirement and yet I'm a nervous wreck. My stomach is upset. My gall bladder is bothering me. A few weeks ago I went to a doctor and got a bill for eighty dollars, and I don't even know what he did. He told me to go home and relax. It was just my nerves. Just my nerves! Tonight for the first time in two weeks I found a little peace. What I saw told me a lot about the turmoil going on inside of me. I wish I could stay this calm, but I know what will happen. Tomorrow I'll be in my car driving, driving. I get caught in traffic. My stomach starts to knot up. I can't relax. When I get home, I don't dare take a drink. My stomach is so bad I tell my wife I don't want anything to eat. Maybe I'll eat later but in the meantime dinner is spoiled. Oh, what's the use? Maybe I need to see a shrink. Maybe he can tell me what's the matter with me. Why can't I find some peace and quiet. Looks like I'm just a victim of the whole darn world."

Perhaps the plane crash he saw was his self-symbol, the symbol of a self torn asunder by lack of inner peace. One reason might be that he was too much possessed by the world, trying so hard to live up to external expectations that he had neglected to find his real self. Now that hidden self was crying out to be heard. He remarked that he had once been a practicing Catholic but had given that up long ago. Religious aspiration shrunk under the pressure of the world. Since his religion was only a function, it was

A Personal Reading of the Cautions of John of the Cross

easily replaced by other, more practical concerns. The trouble was that these concerns had not brought him peace. He now wondered what they were all about. Perhaps this very wondering marks the beginning of a change for the better.

With this occurrence in the background, I can begin to consider St. John's cautions against the world. He says, "In order to free thyself perfectly from the evil which the world can do to thee, thou shalt use three cautions."[13] The words of the first caution are characteristically deep.[14] They invite me to read them thoughtfully, attempting as much as possible to "bracket" my spontaneous prejudices. These arise inevitably from the "ego-orientation" of my culture. It is tempting to read these words as providing me with an "instant technique" for spiritual perfection. Technical service for souls seeking a spiritual life is not what St. John provides. Rather he issues an invitation to me to ready myself for the gift of contemplative union, should God grant this to me. He makes no guarantee. His appeal is not to my will power but to me as the poor man before God who needs all the grace He can give. Weak and sinful though I am, I want to commit myself in faith and dedication to the following of Christ. St. John appeals to that in me which wants to be no more and no less than an instrument of His will. He appeals to that in me which wants to live in this world without being of this world. In the words of the first caution,

St. John tells me that "for all persons thou shalt have equal love and equal forgetfulness, whether they be thy relatives or no, withdrawing thy heart from these as well as from those . . ."

What might this first part of the caution imply for those of us who wish *at the same time* to love and serve the world, as Christ loved and served it, and yet to be able to join with Christ in his condemnation of the world? In other words, how is it possible to live at once in the world with "equal love and equal forgetfulness"?

Remember the man in the meditation class. His life revealed an imbalance where equal love and equal forgetfulness of the world are concerned. He catered to the world so much that he forgot the necessity to condemn it. He stressed involvement to the point of excluding any kind of detachment. Thus in this first caution, St. John reminds us of a fundamental rhythm of the spiritual life: that of involvement and detachment, of being wholly present where I am and at the same time not making my presence there an ultimate concern.

Similarly, my love for relatives and friends, no matter how deep, can never replace the one thing needful: to unite myself with the Father's will for this world. For the sake of my spiritual perfection, I must overcome the attachment I feel for relatives and friends. Any lasting attachment outside of God is a string that ties me down and prevents me from soaring upward. Christ says it drastically.

A Personal Reading of the Cautions of John of the Cross

Anyone who prefers father or mother to me is not worthy of me. Anyone who prefers son or daughter to me is not worthy of me. Anyone who does not take his cross and follow in my footsteps is not worthy of me. Anyone who finds his life will lose it; anyone who loses his life for my sake will find it.[15]

The spiritual man must loosen himself from everything and everyone that is not God. The absence of such dependence and overattachment does not prevent love; rather this kind of emotional independence or forgetfulness of childish emotional ties makes love all the purer. It makes it even possible for me to love my enemies and bless those who would curse me.

St. John is by no means saying that I am to cease caring for my relatives or for those in need; he simply wants me to keep the proper perspective in mind. True Christian love always loves the other in Christ. He is the source of all human love and of all the ways by which I can express this love concretely in my life.

By making God the center of my love, rather than any temporal and passing person or thing, I am able to keep the proper balance where my love relations with others are concerned. When I love in an over-dependent way, I am likely to make this relation an end in itself. Slowly but surely I am drawn out of the true center of my love. When this happens, I have to "forget" my overdependent binding to the other in order to remember that God is the foundation of our love. Love and forgetfulness are thus like two evenly weighted scales that keep me balanced in the center. I do not grant any one person the affection I owe to God alone; I am mindful, however, that my love for God must manifest itself in the love I show toward my fellow man. Human love is then an overflow of the love I reserve wholly for God.

Love of neighbor is not meant to be a vague universal love of which I say that I love everything in general but never show this love to anyone in particular. Christian love is always a directed love. It is directed in accordance with my capacity to give of self in the situation where I happen to be. The fact that my love is limited reminds me that I can do only so much. I need not feel guilty for situations about which I can do nothing. Otherwise I would not be living in equal love and equal forgetfulness.

If I am to incarnate Christ's love in the world, I must extend this love equally to all; at the same time I must recognize that love is limited in its expressiveness in accordance with the circumstances of my life. I must be careful also not to confuse the degree of love with the kind of aid and assistance I can give. A nurse may spend three hours with one patient and five minutes with another. The degree of love in both cases may be equal though circumstances dictate the kind of nursing aid each patient receives.

In the same quote, St. John says that we are to hold those we love, relatives or not, as strangers to us. In this way we will serve them better than by "setting upon them the affection" we owe to God alone.

A Personal Reading of the Cautions of John of the Cross

Between myself and those I love there has to be a relation of caring and not caring. Equally loving them all, I am equally detached from them, for equal love can only be understood in the light of equal forgetfulness. Forgetfulness requires that I give the fullness of my affection and attachment to God alone. I must hold the one I love at a distance from me, lest I forget that we are in the last analysis strangers to one another, known in the fullest sense only to God. To look upon the other as in some essential way a stranger is to look upon him as unique. I must respect the mystery the other is and not settle ultimate affection upon him. I owe such affection only to God. Love for God liberates me to love others as they really are. For it is only God Who knows me as I am and it is only in Him that I am able to love others without making undue emotional demands upon them.

As soon as I make one person the last source of my happiness or joy, I begin to lose my proper relation to God. Moreover, I deceive myself because no person, whether husband, wife, or friend, can ever fully satisfy me. The ultimate fulfillment I seek comes only in union with God. All people, then, are worthy of my love but no person is worthy of *all* my love. The fullness of my love finds its beginning and its end in God.

"Love not one person better than another or thou shalt go astray, for he whom God loves best is worthy to be loved best, and thou knowest not who it is that God best loveth." I do not know who it is that God deems most worthy of my love. God may love a person who in my eyes appears a great sinner. An alcoholic who neglects his family may in his heart not wish to hurt them but he cannot help himself. God understands his good intention and loves him in spite of his weakness. But I cannot see him as God does. From a practical viewpoint, he seems incompetent to me. While I may not trust him with a position of great responsibility, I cannot pass final judgment on him. This right is God's alone.

"But if thou are equally forgetful of them all, as befits thee for holy recollection, thou shalt free thyself from going astray as regards the greater or lesser degree of love due to each." If I am attached to no one, in the sense that God alone is my first and last source of love, I can ready myself for recollection. I let these others fade momentarily into the background and bring myself before the Lord. I am not inclined to show more affection for one than for the other. I have equal love for each because I am equally forgetful of them all. Thus I keep myself from going astray in regard to the degree of love I owe to each. When I love the other in God, I am more sensitive to his needs and less likely to manipulate him to serve my ends alone. Such respectful detachment ought to exist in any true love relationship. It is the main way by which I come to let the other be.

A Personal Reading of the Cautions of John of the Cross

As my love becomes more pure because more centered in God, I cease concentrating on the good or bad qualities people possess: of such matters, St. John says, "Think not of them at all, be they good things or evil things; flee from them in so far as thou fairly canst." This kind of preoccupation with what others do makes it impossible for me to rest with God in holy recollection.

In this style of living in equal love and equal forgetfulness, St. John cautions that the devil will be on the lookout to deceive me. The world too will entrance me to unbounded love of its pleasures and possessions. But I must pay a terrible price if I lose my balance. Remember the man who found himself the possessor of cars and houses and growing bank accounts but sadly felt that life had lost its meaning.

To live in equal love and equal forgetfulness brings with it a special reward: "In doing that which has been described lies security..." St. John does not mean the kind of security that comes with an old age pension or a life insurance policy. I could compare his notion of security with the way a tree is secure in the ground when its roots trail deeply below the surface of the soil. In the same way I will be secure when my roots plunge into the firm ground of my loving surrender to God. In this love relation lies lasting security. In and through it, I disentangle myself from any attachment that may displace my lasting attachment to the eternal.

I am reminded of what Thomas à Kempis said happens when I go out among men. I never return without feeling less of a man.[16] This may seem a harsh statement at first. Am I not a creature of this earth? Is it not in the world that I find the source and meaning of my life? To understand the implications of Thomas' remark, I have to meditate on what a reversal the Revelation offers to the ordinary way I look at things. Ordinarily, I tend to go out into the world to find my meaning as a man. The Revelation teaches that I also go out in the world but I do not make that world my last meaning. When the Christian goes into the world and plunges madly into all its pleasures, projects, and concerns, forgetting that his true home is with the eternal, he is like the prodigal son. He returns from this adventure less of a man and looks to his Father for forgiveness.

Even in a small way, I can get some feeling for what Thomas is stressing in these words: "If you are really aiming at an interior life, a spiritual life, you must be off with Jesus, away from the crowd."[17]

Remember the last time you attended a cocktail party. The noise, the drinks, the smells, the somewhat vapid conversation. "It's been so long since I've seen you. You look marvelous. Can I get you a refill?" And you think, "She's changed so much. For someone who's always dieting, she's put on a lot of weight in the past few months." You move away drink in hand. The pasteboard party smile gets pasted

A Personal Reading of the Cautions of John of the Cross

on your face. There is a sinking feeling in your heart of falseness and superficiality. At long last the evening is over. You gather your belongings and go outside. The fresh air smells so good. You breathe the fresh air in and the phony air out. On the way home you try to gather your *self* together. It has been buried under a pile of cigarette butts, ice cubes, crumbled napkins and left over cheese balls. At the cocktail party, you may come close to losing your center in the crowd.

That my true home is in the world but not of the world affronts my common sense. It is a revelation that easily gets side-tracked in our day. I am always tempted to make the temporal my source of lasting satisfaction. I may identify religion with mere emotional experience. I want to forget the Cross.

Christ died for my sins because He cared first about obeying the Father's will. He did not like the idea of suffering but He bore it in obedience. He knew that this act would make no sense by ordinary standards, but He hoped His disciples at least would listen to the deeper message of His death.

> If you loved me you would have been glad to know that
>   I am going to the Father,
> for the Father is greater than I.[18]

To follow Christ means that in some way I will have to be a paradox like Him. I will have to live in the absurdity of equal love and equal forgetfulness, in the silence of recollected presence to the Father. How absurd such acts will seem to the typical cocktail party crowd and yet they are the truest realities for me as a Christian.

> If the world hates you,
> remember that it hated me before you.
> If you belonged to the world,
> the world would love you as its own;
> but because you do not belong to the world,
> because my choice withdrew you from the world,
> therefore the world hates you.
> Remember the words I said to you:
> A servant is not greater than his master.
> If they persecuted me.
> they will persecute you too;
> if they kept my word,
> they will keep yours as well.
> But it will be on my account that they will do all his,
> because they do not know the one who sent me [9]

In His infinite mercy and love, the Father sent His Son to redeem mankind. His Revelation becomes the light that illuminates the Christian on his journey through this world and toward the Father, in Whom he finds a final resting place.

Closing Prayer

Lord, You lived in equal love and equal forgetfulness. People gathered to hear Your words; yet You

A Personal Reading of the Cautions of John of the Cross

maintained respectful distance from them. When they crowded around You to make You king, You went away and hid Yourself. This action was to show them that no earthly involvement could take precedence over the fulfillment of the Father's will. The source of Your love for men was Your love for the Father. You ask that we love one another, but this love is at times distorted by anger, envy, guilt. Teach me how to love so that I may neither overwhelm the other with my concern nor neglect him in his need. Grant that the grace of Your Holy Spirit may illumine my life so that I may love in a Christian way — equally concerned and equally forgetful. In my forgetfulness of the other, let me remember You as source of his life. In mutual detachment, let us find more intimacy with You. Then our love for one another will be less selfish and more like Your love for us.

> This is my commandment:
> love one another,
> as I have loved you.
> A man can have no greater love
> than to lay down his life for his friends.
> You are my friends,
> if you do what I command you.
> I shall not call you servants any more,
> because a servant does not know
> his master's business;
> I call you friends,
> because I have made known to you
> everything I have learned from my Father.[20]

The Fourth Reading

The sky is clear, the stars are shining, the breeze is biting cold, a perfect end of winter night. It is the first day of the Lenten season. This morning my forehead was signed with ashes. You are dust and unto dust you shall return. Repent and believe in the Good News.

The spiritual writer makes the Good News a reality. In faithfulness to Christ, he makes His words live again in light of his life experience. Reading St. John's second caution against the world is not like reading an abstract theory; it puts me in tune with daily life.

He speaks first "with respect to temporal good things."[2][1] The things that God gives me are good but, if I am to experience their goodness, they must not be isolated from their Giver and made ends in themselves. The beauty of the eternal shines through every temporal thing. All things participate in God's goodness, for in loving concern He creates and maintains each one of them. Anything in isolation from its divine source may become the cause not of goodness but of greedy possessiveness.

"Herein it is needful, if thou wouldst truly free thyself from this kind of evil and moderate the excesses of thine appetite, to abhor all kinds of possession and to have no care for them — neither as

A Personal Reading of the Cautions of John of the Cross

to food, nor clothing, nor any other created thing, nor as to the morrow." St. John calls temporal good things, in isolation from God, an evil. I must direct my care to something higher, to seeking the kingdom of God, and whatever else I need, shall, in His generosity and according to His will, be added to me.

St. John is speaking in this caution to sisters with a solemn vow of poverty, for whom all personal possession was forbidden. They were to abhor all worldly possession in order to free themselves for possession by God alone. Not caring for worldly goods freed them to bind their lives to the eternal source of every temporal thing.

There is also a message in this way of radical dispossession for any one who desires to deepen his spiritual life. I too must become inwardly detached from the person or thing that isolates me from God. I too can enjoy what this world offers while letting go when any worldly good displaces my love for God. The cloistered sister practices detachment by abandoning all personal possession. I cannot do likewise and live in the world, but I can try "to have no care" for my possessions in the sense that I care for material goods without becoming totally absorbed in them.

A family needs certain goods to maintain a style of life compatible with a certain neighborhood and social class. Having these goods is for the family not evil, provided they handle them thoughtfully and recognize when it is necessary to cut back in order not to be possessed by their possessions.

Such cautions may grate on ears accustomed to mass advertising. My materially minded culture trains me to possess things. The media beckons me to buy my ticket to happiness. The commercial society never cautions me against possession. The more you have, the more you want; the more you want, the more you get.

Does material comfort necessarily make me happy? Persons who possess all that money can buy may envy the simple lives of those of modest means while those with few resources may curse the rich. I may measure the value of life by what I have or have not. Either way blinds me to the finiteness of things. I forget their temporality. Care for external things may overwhelm care for my inner life. I am careless about the dimension which matters most. And when the time of my death approaches, I may look around and ask, "Where is the life I have lost in living? Where is the peace of mind I forsook in my efforts to collect as much as I could."[22]

What I am to abhor is not so much the necessities of life, like food, clothing, and shelter. I am to avoid lasting attachment in regard to any of these things. When I see that one thing, or for that matter one person, becomes the beginning and end of my world, I must listen to St. John's caution against the world.

A Personal Reading of the Cautions of John of the Cross

Repeatedly he says, detach yourself from any thing, situation, or person to prevent its becoming so primary that you forget the real situation of your life in relation to Our Lord. Call to mind Christ's regard for the lilies of the field and the birds of the air.

> Look at the birds in the sky. They do not sow or reap or gather into barns; yet your heavenly Father feeds them. Are you not worth much more than they are? ... Think of the flowers growing in the fields; they never have to work or spin; yet I assure you that not even Solomon in all his regalia was robed like one of these. Now if that is how God clothes the grass in the field ... will he not much more look after you ...?[23]

It is not easy to feel this kind of trust in the Father.[24] It is not easy to believe that He cares for me more than for plants and animals. It is especially not easy to have this total trust in Him when my desires are not fulfilled and what I need is not forthcoming. My inclination is to worry excessively about the morrow. Sensible planning is fine. I have to gather the harvest into barns, but my tendency is to go overboard. To say I trust in God and at the same time to act as if created things will insure my happiness. I want to organize my life in such a way that my future is secure. I act as if I have to control the world. But really I have nothing to say about it. He alone knows what is best for me to reach my destiny.

Complete trust in the all caring will of the Father is hard to come by in this age. I am more prone to trust myself and relinquish trust in God. Yet this same age that tempts me to rely on material things only is the testing ground for faith. The more the things of the world beseech me to forget the Divine, the more I am called to dwell anew on my finitude. The most affluent society materialistically may be the most poor spiritually. Yet it is this same society that reveals to me the foolishness of such a position. I now know from experience that I have to direct my concern higher. Mere material things do not suffice to fulfill me spiritually.

Witness the rapid rise and fall of many enterprises. Only His word does not pass away.[25] Watch the quick decay of many products famous six months ago. Only His word does not pass away. I throw out things that promised to make me happy. These things come and go. Only His word does not pass away. All those things that used to delight me may in the end disappoint me. More than ever I am mindful that I have to align myself with His kingdom. All else is secondary to this. If I am sincerely on the way toward Him, He will not fail me. He is always there when I need Him most. He hears my cry and brings me the comfort I seek. If I continue looking for Him, though the world cast countless obstacles in my path, I shall not fail to find Him. If I go to Him, St. John writes, the rest that I seek shall be added unto me.

A Personal Reading of the Cautions of John of the Cross

His grace comes to me as pure gift, a gift of love and concern. "For He that cares for the beasts will not be forgetful of thee."

God is always waiting for me. I can go away from Him for many years. I can close Him out of my life. Then one day I may call His name. He comes to me as if there had never been a separation between us. Silence is not separation. He did not forget me, though He allowed me to be forgetful of Him.

In the movie *Ben Hur,* Hur, on his way to captivity in Rome, is dying of thirst. He drops near a well and is given a cup of water by a kind man. They look at each other for a brief moment. This look pierces the heart of Ben Hur, though he does not know how deep. He forgets it. The look in those compassionate eyes is buried deep within him, to be remembered on a future day. Years later, he returns to the Holy Land, filled with bitterness against his captors. His one thought is to seek revenge. By coincidence he happens to be in Jerusalem the day a man is to be crucified — a Nazarene accused of trying to incite a revolution. The evidence is not too clear. He watches this gentle looking man carry his cross. His frail body shrinks under its weight. Hur tries to help him but is pushed back by the guards. He follows the mob to the hill where the man is to be put to death. He is there in the crowd at the hour of the crucifixion. Jesus looks down at his enemies and utters words that could only come from God. "Father, forgive them;

they do not know what they are doing."[26] Hur remembers now who he is. This is the same man who took pity on him when he was thirsty. His compassion is so great that he can forgive his accusers. At that moment, Hur felt the sword lifted from his heart. No longer would the need for vengeance torment him. He would remember instead the gentleness of this man who loved his enemies and did good to those who persecuted him. Hur was free not only physically but spiritually as well.

"In this way," St. John says, "shalt thou attain silence and peace in the senses." More often than not such peace eludes me. My eyes dart from one desired thing to the next. My hands become grasping when they should be receiving. Not only are my outer eyes restless; my inner eyes are darting about as well. I am blinded by my efforts to save myself. As long as my inner eyes do not dwell upon the Light that illumines the world, I will be restless. Silence and peace find no place in my senses. Still the promise of peace persists if I dispose myself outwardly and inwardly to receive it.

> I have told you all this
> so that you may find peace in me.
> In the world you will have trouble,
> but be brave:
> I have conquered the world.[27]

Christ's promise of peace is ever faithful. His grace

A Personal Reading of the Cautions of John of the Cross

works in such mysterious ways that peace can come to me even if I am undeserving of it. Nonetheless, I shall be more ready to receive this gift when, through His grace, I open my heart to God and prepare a place for His presence.

Closing Prayer

Preserve me, Lord, from the dangers of possession so that I may see Your countenance in the eyes of every person, Your caring hand sustaining all things. Let my inner eyes be so restful that their restfulness pervades my outer eyes as well. In that way I may attain peace in senses, mind, and spirit. You promise me peace. Not worldly contentment, not freedom from suffering, but peace. Help me not to be embittered if I fail to attain those things I think will make me happy. Let me see in this failure a sign of Your love for me. Perhaps it is worldly unhappiness that in the deepest sense prepares me to receive Your spiritual peace. Saintly people are not strangers to suffering. They have endured physical pain; they have seen empires collapse, yet none of this worldly unhappiness disturbed their inner peace. It was as if they heard You say, "Start fresh again."

In all my striving for peace, Lord, let me keep a balance of doing and being. There shall be the doing, for the Christian is a man of action, and there shall be the standing back in appreciation for what has been done. This is the moment of recollection I often neglect in my urge to push ahead. I neglect to pause and see my work in Your light. At the end of every sentence there is a period, a natural pause, to look back over what has been said, to see if it makes sense. My daily life must include similar periods of rest — not to act but to enjoy, not to do but to recollect what I have done. For recollection alerts me to the real meaning of my action. Once I begin to enjoy Your divine presence in all things, I can no longer worship them in isolation from their Source. I can no longer be a victim of my possessions. If You give me good health, success, a fine job, ownership of property, You give these gifts out of love. They manifest Your love for me but they are passing. What lasts is Your love. In this light, things lose their power to possess me. I possess them not for themselves but in so far as they remind me of Your loving presence in this world.

Grant, O Lord, that my inner eyes may see Your light. That my inner ears may hear Your word. That my inner voice may answer Your call to everlasting joy.

The Fifth Reading

I sit here this evening listening to the wind blowing through the branches of barren trees. The wind, blowing here and there, seems lacking in direction. It

A Personal Reading of the Cautions of John of the Cross

is like the words I sometimes hear. Are they words or just sounds empty of real meaning? Some words are spoken with lips alone; they do not tell us what is happening in a person's heart. Such chatter may at times betray a lack of inwardness. Too often my words simply fill up the silence. Often they are not words of charity and compassion but of cynicism and spite. Such words do not heal; they cause further pain.

Through my words I relate to other people. The ideal is to use words in such a way that they express my respect for others in their suffering and joy. Such is the ideal but what is the reality? Gossipy words. Greedy words. Words that meddle and mind the business of others. Envious words. Seductive words. So many words and so little respect.

How different from my empty words are the full words of the spiritual master. His words are never meant to be abusive, though I may be offended by them. If I listen well, however, I shall find that his words are faithful to the Gospel message. They are filled with respect and love, the hallmarks of Christian community.

Interestingly enough, St. John's third caution against the world deals with the problem of communication in a Christian community.

> The third caution is very necessary if thou art to learn to guard thyself in the convent from all evil with respect to

the religious. Many, through not observing it, have not only lost the peace and blessing of their souls, but have fallen, and habitually fall, into many evils and sins. This caution is that thou shouldst keep thyself with all diligence from setting thy thoughts upon what happens in the community, and still more from speaking of it; which may concern, or may have concerned, some religious in particular: thou shalt not speak of his character, or of his manner of life, or of any of his business, however grave it be, either under pretext of zeal or of desire to remedy matters, save to that person to whom it is right that thou shouldst speak of it at the appointed time. Nor shouldst thou ever be shocked or marvel at aught that thou seest or hearest, but shouldst strive to keep thy soul in forgetfulness of it all.[28]

Though he directs his words to the Discalced Carmelite nuns of Beas, their meaning extends far beyond this convent and becomes an invitation to consider the more universal implications of communication and community. He says this third caution is necessary if the sisters are to learn to guard themselves in the convent from all evil with respect to religious. The caution is equally applicable to my relations with those I encounter in daily life.

Guarding myself against evil in regard to others implies guarding my intentions. I ought to will the good of the other in accordance with the word of God, though I may fail at times to live up to this intention because of the obstacles in my way: my penchant for disrespect, the hours I may spend in idle chatter, the empty gossip that mars the other's reputation. All of these evils are obstacles to willing and doing the good in my dealings with others.

An old but true adage is that "the road to hell is paved with good intentions." I have to evaluate what I am really after. Are my strivings only in accord with what *I* call good? Or are they in tune with the Divine Word? "Many, through not observing it [this caution], have not only lost the peace and blessing of their souls, but have fallen, and habitually fall, into many evils and sins."

St. John is talking to me when he says this. I have attempted to obey the word of the Lord but often I have substituted for this word my own desires. Not only have I fallen once: I have fallen "habitually" into evils and sins, not the least of which are sins against Christian communication. Christ spoke what the Father wanted Him to say and as He was supposed to say it.

> For what I have spoken does not come from myself;
> no, what I was to say, what I had to speak,
> was commanded by the Father who sent me,
> and I know that his commands mean eternal life.
> And therefore what the Father has told me
> is what I speak.[29]

To follow the way of Christian communication Our Lord exemplified, I have to begin by listening to the will of God in y personal life. Then, out of this solitary listening, I can strive to communicate His word to others. What inspires people is not so much the words I speak but the way I am when I speak them.

". . . thou shouldst keep thyself with all diligence from setting thy thoughts upon what happens in the community and still more from speaking of it . . ." St. John is speaking here to persons who are overly preoccupied with what others are doing instead of quietly living their lives in union with God. Instead of examining their own conscience, they are only too ready to criticize others. Rather than correcting their own faults, they are intent upon rectifying the misdeeds of others. This kind of disrespectful behavior is not confined to religious community. I'm often caught in the same pattern. How often do I judge others instead of attempting to improve myself. Playing God in this way, I place myself above others. I grow proud not humble. The exalted position I take on is easily threatened. As soon as I place myself above others, I begin to compare myself with them. My privileged position grows shaky every time I discover that the other is better than I, if only in little things.[30]

"She dresses better than I. Beside her I look shabby. She got four phone calls today. I didn't get any. What time will she be home? She's bound to come in later than I. Where does she get the energy? I can't do half the amount of work she does. When did she buy that new car? My old jalopy looks sick next to her new model."

With such thoughts running around in my head, there is less chance that I can really listen to the will of God. I am too caught in self-interest. I am so absorbed in following these fleeting thoughts that I am carried away from my center. So attached am I to what is not God that I no longer listen to His word. He usually communicates Himself to me in silence, but how can I expect to hear when I am never still enough to listen?

Not only must I keep my mind uncluttered by such concerns; I must also cease speaking of them. For my seeming concern for others may be in reality a betrayal of charity. Such concern is not a true overflow of love for the other out of love for God. I simply try to satisfy my curiosity or to air my anger, jealousy, and hurt pride.

"I guess you'll be late this evening." Such a simple statement may show my concern that she is going to be out long after dark or it may be a way of finding out where she is going. Curiosity is easily disguised as concern. But unlike love, which respects the other, curiosity reduces the other to an object, to a puzzle to be solved.

St. John does not mince words in his admonition against such curious concern: ". . . thou shalt not speak of his character, or of his manner of life, or of any of his business, however grave it be . . ."

What is a person's character? Often what is called my character is no more than the public image others have of me. Sometimes this image is like the person I am, but this is not always the case. No outsider knows me in my inmost self as God does. How then can another judge my character in an ultimate sense? This is impossible and hence St. John says, it is best not to speak publicly of one another's character. Privately I may feel there are some discrepancies in your behavior. I can reflect on these alone or in confidence with a trusted friend. But to make your character an object of public surveillance, to stick you with a reputation that may not at all accord with the person you are, to sit in judgment upon you — all of these so-called concerns are to be cautioned against.

Nor may I speak of your manner of life. It may well be that your style of life offends my own standards. Your way of doing things may not at all be in accord with my ideal of what should be done. Nonetheless the respect I have for you as a person must go deeper than my affinity for the way you live or the manner of life you exemplify. Generally it is best, as St. John says, not to speak of a person's manner of life or his character or his business, no matter how serious my concern may be. This kind of speaking degenerates often into unfounded gossip that may falsify this person's position in life. It is best that I guard my tongue and leave such talk to the discretion of the spiritual master or whoever is delegated with authority.

I need to be cautioned in this regard, for I tend to speak too easily about others "under the pretext of zeal or of desire to remedy matters." The do-gooder does not necessarily have the other's best interest at heart.

St. John adds that we are not to speak of these things among one another, that is, cafeteria style. However, if I am convinced in conscience that another's manner of life seriously endangers others, I can communicate my concern to the person to whom it is right to speak "at the appointed time." Such a respectful approach to the person is different from the usual gossipy way. In the latter case I might mar his reputation without having real evidence at hand. All I draw upon is the false witness of my assumptions.

Christian communication implies prayerful surrender to the word of God speaking in self and others. Out of this respectful openness will emerge the wisdom to know when to speak and when to be silent. And, when I have to speak, to speak wisely and moderately to the appropriate person. In persistently trying to see the other against the background of the Sacred, I shall better preserve inner peace. In such peace of soul, I am less likely to be "shocked" or to "marvel" at anything I see or hear. Instead of dramatizing out of proportion every event, "strive to keep thy soul in forgetfulness of it all."

Forgetfulness is not indifference or lack of concern. It marks a person willing to be silent about another's mistake and not call attention to himself by telling an enticing story at his expense. What I try to forget are the superficial diagnoses made by idle gossipers, the innuendos of people consumed by curiosity, the excuses they use to belittle others. I try as well to forget my hurt pride, the times I've been jealous, the irritation and antipathy I've felt. Christian forgetfulness is the willingness to turn the other cheek when someone I trusted betrays me. It means seeing behind nasty remarks the loneliness of a man without friends, behind envy a girl who has lost self-respect, behind violence a fellow deprived of genuine love.

Closing Prayer

O Lord, in my everyday dealings with fellow men, I often fail to follow the example of Your loving compassion. You always tried to see the good in even the worst of sinners. You warned us not to judge lest we be judged, yet how often I pass sentence on someone who has lost my favor. Seldom do I wait for the "appointed time" to speak or the right person to whom to make known my concern. Rather I speak to

A Personal Reading of the Cautions of John of the Cross

the person next door or the ones with whom I lunch — as if the person I'm talking about were simply a commodity on the marketplace whose value we cleverly debate. To cure this disrespect, I have to be guided by Your example. Often those who had lost their reputation in the eyes of the community gained Your friendship and were reformed by Your forgiving word. With Your help and grace perhaps my words can become an expression of my intent to will the good. Then I will less readily fall into the evils of false communication.

Lord, I am weak in this endeavor to use words well. If my words are to be true expressions of my deepest self, I have to learn how to listen. Only when I listen can I truly speak. Listening to the voice of the Spirit Who speaks within me prompts me not to engage in idle gossip. It allows me to address the other out of respect for his integrity. Teach me to listen. Help me hold my speaking until I have learned to listen to Your spirit in silence. Help me to cease conversing until I have gathered together the words I want to say, words that emerge not from my cleverness but from Your compassion.

I am reminded of Your servant, St. Seraphim, who for many years lived in the silent wilderness of Russia praying ceaselessly. Only after many years of listening did he feel ready to speak. The words he said were few but people flocked from miles around simply to hear the sound of his voice. His voice had become a channel for the Holy Spirit. The words that rose out of his solitude were words of truth. When his audience heard them, they were touched. Hardened hearts awakened. Hearts of stone became fertile soil for truths of the Spirit. When St. Seraphim spoke of the joy that was his from having lived in solitude, the persons who heard him felt their hearts leap with a joy like his.

Such speaking is the core of Christian communication. Though I may never achieve such depth of listening, I ask, O Lord, that in all my endeavors to communicate I may be ever mindful of this message from the life of St. Seraphim: that only he who listens can truly speak; that only he who dwells in silence will have something of value to say.

The Sixth Reading

Today is the first day of spring. I awoke at sunrise, parted the curtains beside my bed and looked out on a bright new morning. The silence was broken sweetly by the sound of chirping birds. In the distance I heard the hum of steady traffic, the slamming of car doors as early risers went to work. A feeling of joy welled up within me. I praised God for giving me another day: this day on which to renew my gratitude for His loving guidance of my life. I had another chance to say thanks and to be mindful, especially during this Lenten season, of my need to repent. I would repent

A Personal Reading of the Cautions of John of the Cross

not just for those obvious faults, present to my consciousness, but for those hidden wrongs that go unnoticed by me but betray a self-preoccupation isolated from the example of Our Lord.

I lay there a few minutes more, thanking God for the gift of this perfect day. I asked Him to be present in my words and my deeds as I arose to join other commuters on the way to work. Today, however, I wanted to be mindful of my fellow men in a way more like that of my Lord. Such thoughts were with me then and are with me now as I begin this evening's reflection.

I continue to wonder at the wisdom St. John displays in describing relations with people. His words ring as true today as when they were written centuries ago.[31] For what he articulates are laws and dynamics so fundamental to the spiritual life that they cannot fail to communicate truths for every age. He is wise enough to know, however, that I may fail to understand what he writes. He says, in effect, if you desire to consider any of these things — that is, what happens in community with others, where you set your thoughts, what you say under pretext of zeal or out of a genuine desire to help — then you will find something wrong even if you "live among angels." This remark emphasizes how often I conclude that something is amiss because I lack the proper understanding of what is being done or said. The same happens when I am unable or in too much of a hurry to consider properly the spiritual knowledge and advice St. John is imparting. I come thus to a faulty judgment.

I may be foolish enough to think I can grasp on first reading the full depth of what he is saying. In my arrogance, I may boast that I understand the substance of his message after only a few moments of cursory reflection. Reading a spiritual writer is not as easy as that. He is communicating on so many levels of meaning that I have to return to his words again and again. Even then I may barely tap the treasure of insight they hold. What the spiritual writer is saying echoes with wisdom and experience that may keep on reverberating in my life long after I cease meditative dwelling on his words. The substance of them stays alive and lives on in me whenever God gives me the grace to be truly present to them.

It is also clear that rational intellect alone cannot pierce the depth of wisdom in these words. The saint appeals not merely to my reason but to those dimensions of life where reason must give way to faith. To relive the saint's words in my life, they must be approached with an attitude of faith. Faith is the leap beyond the barrier where logic fears to go. So understanding the substance of the saint's words is a process of abiding reflection — but not the kind of reflection characteristic of reason alone. What is required is a meditative or participative reflection, a reliving in faith of the saint's words in the day to day unfolding of our lives.[32]

St. John continues his cautions against the world by considering what happened to Lot's wife, who "because she was troubled at the perdition of the Sodomites and looked backward to see what was happening, was punished by God, who turned her into a statue of salt." Lot's wife was more interested in the fate of these sinners than in following God's command. She should have been forgetful of them and focused only on obeying the will of God. Similarly, St. John tells the sisters, when you see bad business in the monastery do not look back at such doings. Even if you live among devils, God wills you to live among them in such a way that you do not look back in thought at their antics but "abandon them wholly, striving to keep thy soul pure and sincere with God, undisturbed by thoughts either of one thing or another."

What St. John says seems relevant to me in regard to the problem of looking back into my own past. I may focus inordinately on it to the neglect of the present moment. In some sense, I am not to look back. It is better to keep my thoughts centered on God's will for me in the present than to be unduly perturbed by what I have or have not done in the past. Especially if I have confessed my faults and received forgiveness, it is unwise to review them scrupulously. God allows me to be in this place now, trying my best to obey Him, and so this is where I belong. Likewise I must try not to center my thoughts on the business of others but to live a more recollected life. Listening to God's will in the events of daily life, I am less likely to be distracted by "this or that." Binding myself to His word makes it easier to retain inner equanimity in the midst of business dealings and inevitable bickerings. The true self, in its inner detachment, centers on the one thing necessary — surrender to God's will. This kind of centered presence allows all dimensions of life to fall into proper order.

In his genuine understanding of human nature, St. John admits that no community of men, just as no individual, will be without some occasion for stumbling. There are never wanting those forces of evil, both inner and outer, that strive to weaken the quest for holiness. When others fall I am not to fret excessively over it. It's as normal for them to fall as for me, for we are all sinners in need of redemption. God permits this kind of stumbling in order to exercise and prove me. This kind of testing helps me to come to a deeper spiritual life. Testing makes me all the more mindful of my need for forgiveness. It proves to me the error of trying to build a spiritual life on my own merits without God's grace. In solitude I reach the depth of my sinfulness together with the discovery of my dependence on Christ.

A Personal Reading of the Cautions of John of the Cross

If I can attain holy detachment and holy recollection — the two attitudes that lead to solitude — and emerge from this experience purified and renewed, then the promise of my Lord is clear.

> I shall not call you servants any more,
> because a servant does not know
> his master's business;
> I call you friends,
> because I have made known to you
> everything I have learned from my Father.[33]

If I can commit myself to the truth His promise holds, I can rejoice and be glad for the hour of salvation is at hand. If I do not listen to "the Spirit of truth who issues from the Father,"[34] then I must face the consequences of my refusal. "... however good may be thy aim and however great thy zeal, the devil will entrap thee either in one place or in another..." Forgetful of my nothingness and God's allness, I shall identify salvation with a time or a place or a person. What happens then is clear. St. John says I shall not only be entrapped; I shall be "securely entrapped," distracted from my true aim in a multitude of ways.

Often lurking beneath my noblest attempts to get involved with others is the suspicion that if I try hard enough I can save others and myself. Even if I overcome my individual ego, I may do so in a false way by attaching myself to the collective ego of the

APPROACHING THE SACRED

group. Now the belief is that "we together" can do it. In both cases, the ego still has me securely entrapped.

Finally, at the end of his cautions against the world, St. John asks that I consider the words of the apostle Saint James: " 'If any man thinketh himself to be a religious, bridling not his tongue, this man's religion is vain'." And immediately, St. John adds, we are to bridle our tongue no less inwardly than outwardly.

I do as much wrong in speaking about others outwardly as in speaking about them inwardly. In both instances I must abandon wholly such preoccupation with others, neither justifying nor accusing them. Expending excessive mental and emotional energy diminishes my availability for tranquil presence to the Divine. It is this presence above all that St. John wants me to devote myself to. Every caution is meant to prepare me for this encounter with my Lord. Whatever the cost, nothing must interfere with this, my first concern. Otherwise my spirituality will be in vain.

Inward speech, especially prayer, ought ideally to be the source of outward speech. What I communicate then does not emerge simply out of my clever manipulating head but out of my humble receptive heart. I may not have all the answers, but I can share with others the questions persons everywhere ask about the spiritual life. What I am seeking is the

A Personal Reading of the Cautions of John of the Cross

union of inner and outer speech, the rhythm of recollection and action, or solitude and togetherness. This union of head and heart is not attained without some effort on my part, an effort marked not by violence but by gentleness.[35]

Many times I am at war within. This inner war of wits and words communicates itself outwardly in agitation, nervousness, unhappiness, loss of serenity. Much as I might like to attain inner and outer peace, it seems as if I am always on the way toward it. Still it is not success that counts but the relaxed intention at least to try. Jesus, after all, promises that what I seek shall be given to me.

> Peace I bequeath to you,
> my own peace I give you,
> a peace the world cannot give, this is my gift to you.[36]

When my heart has surrendered to Him in all things, my inner peace of presence cannot help but show itself outwardly.

> I give you a new commandment:
> love one another;
> just as I have loved you,
> you also must love one another.
> By this love you have for one another,
> everyone will know that you are my disciples.[37]

My very being will radiate the inner peace I experience in His presence. This peace is what others remember most of all.

My hope is to reach, with God's grace, that longed for time here or hereafter, when all that I say and do will be an embodiment of His eternal, infinite love for man and world. This is why He gave me life; this is what I am here for.

Closing Prayer

O Lord, I long for the peace You promise. Too often I experience my inner life torn apart by concerns for this or that. What shall I say? Where shall I go? What shall I do? I ask these questions in such a tight and tense way you would think the world awaited their answer. Yet I know this is not so.

Why is it when I long for peace I do so little to let Your promise come true in my life? I continue along the path of fragmentation and illusion. I build up my ego by trying to solve the difficulties of daily life without recourse to Your help. Why is it when I long to realize the promise of Your peace in my life, I still persist in my old ways, refusing to put on the new man? I say I want to pray, but I'm too busy now. I'll pray some other day. Surely this is no way to let Your promise come true. I am aware of the many times I fall, have fallen, and will fall. But when I say to You "Abba Father," You hear my prayer and send as my comforter Your Holy Spirit, as my pattern Your Beloved Son.

A Personal Reading of the Cautions of John of the Cross

Father, Son and Spirit, aid me in my quest for peace. Help me to heal the fragmentation of this frantic life. Let me escape the clutch of my own ego control. Only then, Lord, shall I find the peace I so ardently seek.

You gave us the words of eternal life. You taught us how to pray for peace. Hallowed be Thy name, Father in heaven. May Thy kingdom on earth be as real for me now as it shall be hereafter. May I do Your will in this life as I desire to do it in the life to come. Though I may forget to ask You, sustain me with the daily bread of life that comes to me through the words of the sacred writers. Though I am unworthy, I ask Your forgiveness for the times I have done things against You. In thankfulness to You for this forgiveness, I shall do my best to extend forgiveness to my fellow men. Most of all, Father, guide me along the path of salvation. Deliver me out of the bondage of iniquity, my own and that of those persons and events that block my passage to You. Whenever I do get lost, grant me a little light by which to return to Your dwelling place with no further delay. I ask these favors not because I deserve them, but because I know that without Your grace I am incapable of finding my way. Guided by Your light, then, I can sing Your praises with the spiritual master, bearing a message not of regret but of joy, not of sorrow but of thanksgiving.

FOOTNOTES

INTRODUCTION

1. Luke 13:24. All quotes from Holy Scripture are taken from *The Jerusalem Bible,* Reader's Edition (Garden City, New York: Doubleday & Company, Inc., 1971).

2. *The Life of Teresa of Jesus,* trans. and ed. E. Allison Peers (Garden City, New York: Image Books, 1960), p. 362.

PART ONE

1. These distinctions are clearly described by Peter-Thomas Rohrbach, in *Conversation with Christ: An Introduction to Mental Prayer* (Denville, N.J.; Dimension Books, 1973). The distinction and correlation between meditation and spiritual reading is also discussed by Eugene Boylan, O. Cist. in *This Tremendous Lover* (Westminster, Maryland: The Newman Press, 1947), pp. 99-112.

2. Rohrbach, pp. 79-84. The second part of this book emerged from regular meditative reading of the *Cautions* of St. John of the Cross.

3. "... mental prayer, in my view, is nothing but friendly intercourse, and frequent solitary converse, with Him Who we know loves us." *The Life of Teresa of Jesus,* p. 110.

4. In his book *The Intellectual Life,* trans. Mary Ryan (Cork: The Mercier Press, 1948), pp. 152-157, A.D. Sertillanges, O.P. distinguishes four kinds of reading: *fundamental, ac-*

Footnotes

cidental, stimulating or *edifying,* and *recreative.* These readings must be regulated and each kind requires a particular approach on the part of the reader.

5. Suggested readings in these areas are indicated on the reading list that follows Part Two.

6. For example, *The Autobiography of St. Thérèse of Lisieux;* St. Francis de Sales, *Introduction to the Devout Life;* St. John of the Cross, *Living Flame of Love.* See reading list for further information.

7. *Living Flame of Love,* trans. and ed. E. Allison Peers (Garden City, New York: Image Books, 1962), pp. 27-28 All quotes from *Living Flame of Love* are taken from this edition, published by arrangement with the Newman Press. That I have chosen to read St. John does not imply that his works are the best place for the beginner to start a spiritual reading program. In fact many spiritual directors caution novices not to read St. John since his writings presuppose a certain advancement in the spiritual life See, for example, Francis Libermann, C.S.Sp., *Spiritual Letters to Clergy and Religious,* Volume Two (Pittsburgh, Pa.. Duquesne University Press, 1964), pp. 235-244. Father Libermann writes to Paul Carron, "I believe that St. John of the Cross was very much enlightened by God, and that all he says is wonderful. But I also believe that our divine Master is still more wonderful; and what we learn from Him is more beautiful, more luminous, and more sanctifying for our souls" (p. 237). Father Libermann also warns his confrere against the danger of illusions and how these might be evoked by what one reads. With his advice in mind, it is possible to read St. John in a more humble way, recognizing the depth of his message and that simply reading it does not mean I am "there."

8. *Living Flame of Love,* p. 148.

9. "Prologue:: Maxims and Sentences," p. 218. All quotes from the *Cautions, Spiritual Sentences and Maxims,* and of St. John of the Cross are "Points of Love" taken from *The Complete Works of Saint John of the Cross,* Volume Three, trans. and ed. E. Allison Peers (Westminster, Maryland: The Newman Press, 1935).

10. 1 Corinthians 2: 1-5.

11. "Prologue: Maxims and Sentences," p. 218.

12. *Living Flame of Love,* p. 131.

13. St. John of the Cross, *Ascent of Mount Carmel,* trans. and ed. E. Allison Peers, Garden City, New York: Image Books, 1958), p. 13. All quotes from the *Ascent of Mount Carmel* are taken from this edition, published by special arrangement with the Newman Press.

14. St. John of the Cross, *Spiritual Canticle,* trans. and ed. E. Allison Peers (Garden City, New York: Image Books, 1961), pp. 40-41.

15. "Maxims and Sentences," No. 5, p. 219.

16. *Ibid.,* No. 7.

17. An unprepared master, however, can be a great hindrance to an initiate's spiritual growth. See *Living Flame of Love,* pp. 100-126.

18. 1 Corinthians 1:18-25.

19. *Ascent of Mount Carmel,* p. 374.

20. See Bernard of Clairvaux, *On the Song of Songs I*, trans. Kilian Walsh, O.C.S.O. (Spencer, Mass.: Cistercian Publications, 1971).

21. Of these fifteen minutes Baron Friedrich von Hügel said to his niece that that daily quarter of an hour, for forty years or more, was one of the greatest sustenances and sources of calm for his life. See *Letters from Baron Friedrich von Hügel to a Niece*, ed. Gwendolen Green (London: J.M. Dent, 1928), p. 119.

22. John 6: 37-38.

23. *Living Flame of Love*, p. 79.

24. Sir Thomas Browne, *Religio Medici*, ed. Jean-Jacques Denonain (Cambridge: The University Press, 1955), p. 102.

25. T.S. Eliot, *Ash Wednesday*, in T.S. Eliot, *Selected Poems*, Harbrace Paperbound Library (New York: Harcourt, Brace & World, Inc., 1934(, pp. 92-93.

26. T.S. Eliot, "East Coker," in T.S. Eliot, *Four Quartets*, a Harvest Book (New York: Harcourt, Brace & World, Inc., 1943), pp. 28-29. Eliot says in the same poem on p. 31:

>   And what there is to conquer
> By strength and submission, has already been discovered
> Once or twice, or several times, by men whom one cannot hope
> To emulate — but there is no competition —
> There is only the fight to recover what has been lost
> And found and lost again and again: and now, under conditions
> That seem unpropitious. But perhaps neither gain nor loss.

For us, there is only the trying. The rest is not our business.

27. See Aldous Huxley, *The Devils of Loudun* (New York: Harper & Row, 1952), pp. 317-320.

28. Søren Kierkegaard, *Purity of Heart Is to Will One Thing*, trans. Douglas V. Steere (New York: Harper & Row, 1956), p. 191.

29. *Ibid.*, p. 190.

30. See Adrian van Kaam, *Personality Fulfillment in the Religious Life* (Denville, N.J.: Dimension Books, Inc., 1967), pp. 103-122.

31. See D d F.K. Steindl-Rast, O.S.B., "Contemplative Community," in *Contemplative Community: A Symposium*, ed. M. Basil Pennington, O.C.S.O. (Washington, D.C.: Cistercian Publications Consortium Press, 1972), pp. 293-298.

32 Psalm 8: 1-4.

33. Pslam 130: 1-2.

34. *Ascent of Mount Carmel*, p. 93

35. *Ibid.*, p. 301.

36. See 2 Peter 1: 304

37. Luke 12:31.

38. "Points of Love," No. 42, p 230.

39. *Ibid.*

40. "Maxims and Sentences," No. 1, p. 219.

41. "Points of Love," No. 42, p. 230.

42. Søren Kierkegaard, *The Point of View for My Work as an Author,* trans. Walter Lowrie (New York, Harper & Row, 1962), pp. 121-138.

43. Dag Hammarskjöld, *Markings,* trans. Lief Sjöberg and W.H. Auden (London: Faber & Faber, 1964), p. 34.

44. "Points of Love," No. 42, p. 230.

45. *Ibid.*

46. *Ibid.*

47. Revelation 5:13.

PART TWO

1. All quotes are taken from the *Cautions* of St. John of the Cross, Volume Three of *The Complete Works of Saint John of the Cross,* trans. and ed. E. Allison Peers (Westminster, Maryland: The Newman Press, 1935), pp. 199-205.

2. "Cautions," p. 199.

3. *Ibid.*

4. *Ibid.*

5. See *Ascent of Mount Carmel*, pp. 68-73.

6. "Cautions," p. 199.

7. John 16:33.

8. Romans 7: 18-19.

9. Philosophical and theological studies too numerous to mention have grappled with the problem of evil and the life-negating power of the demonic. One recent and valuable study is that by Paul Ricoeur, *The Symbolism of Evil* (New York: Harper & Row, 1967).

10. John 14:19-20.

11. See Bert van Croonenburg, *Don't Be Discouraged* (Denville, N.J.: Dimension Books, Inc., 1972).

12. "Cautions," p. 199.

13. *Cautions,* "Against the World," p. 199.

14. The first caution is that for all persons thou shalt have equal love and equal forgetfulness, whether they be thy relatives or no, withdrawing thy heart from these as much as from those; more so, indeed, in some ways, from thy kinsmen, lest flesh and blood quicken with natural love, which is ever alive among kinsfolk, the which thou must ever mortify for the sake of spiritual perfection. Hold them all as strangers to thee; in this way thou dost serve them better than by setting upon them the affection which thou owest to God. Love not one person better than another or thou shalt go astray, for he whom God loves best is worthy to be loved best, and thou knowest not who it is that God best loveth. But if thou are equally

forgetful of them all, as befits thee for holy recollection, thou shalt free thyself from going astray as regards the greater or lesser degree of love due to each. Think not of them at all, be they good things or evil things; flee from them in so far as thou fairly canst. And, if thou observe not this, thou hast not learned to be a religious, neither shalt be able to attain to holy recollection, nor to free thyself from the imperfections that come to thee hereby. And, if in this matter thou desire to allow thyself a certain licence, the devil will deceive thee in one way or another, or thou wilt deceive thyself, under some colour of good or of evil. In doing that which has been described lies security, for in no other way canst thou free thyself from the imperfections and evils which the soul obtains from creatures. "Caution the First," p. 200.

15. Matthew 10: 37-39.

16. See Thomas à Kempis, *The Imitation of Christ,* trans. Ronald Knox and Michael Oakley (New York: Sheed and Ward, 1960).

17. *Ibid,* p. 43.

18. John 14:28.

19. John 15: 18-21.

20. John 15: 12-15.

21. The second caution against the world is with respect to temporal good things. Herein it is needful, if thou wouldst truly free thyself from this kind of evil and moderate the excesses of thine appetite, to abhor all kinds of possession and to have no care for them — neither as to food, nor clothing, nor any other created thing, nor as to the

morrow. Thou must direct this care to something higher, namely, to seeking the kingdom of God — that is, to not failing God — and the rest, as His Majesty says, shall be added unto us. For He that cares for the beasts will not be forgetful of thee. In this way shalt thou attain silence and peace in the senses. "Caution the Second," pp. 200-201.

22. These questions were inspired by the following lines from T.S. Eliot's poem *Choruses from 'The Rock'*: "Where is the Life we have lost in living? / Where is the wisdom we have lost in knowledge?" *Selected Poems*, p. 107.

23. Matthew 6: 26-30.

24. "But you, you must not set your hearts on things to eat and things to drink, nor must you worry. It is the pagans of this world who set their hearts on all these things. Your Father well knows you need them. No; set your hearts on his kingdom, and these other things will be given you as well." Luke 12: 29-31.

25. "I tell you solemnly, before this generation has passed away all these things will have taken place. Heaven and earth will pass away, but my words will never pass away." Matthew 24: 34-35.

26. Luke 23:34.

27. John 16:33.

28. "Caution the Third," p. 201.

29. John 12: 49-50.

30. For a study of the dynamics of envious comparison, see Adrian van Kaam, *Envy and Originality* (Garden City,

New York: Doubleday & Company, Inc., 1972), pp. 10-14.

31. The second part of the third caution, that is the basis for this reflection reads: For if thou desirest to consider any of these things, even though thou live among angels, many things in them will seem to thee to be amiss, since thou wilt not understand the substance of them. Take thou here for an example Lot's wife, who, because she was troubled at the perdition of the Sodomites and looked backward to see what was happening, was punished by God, who turned her into a statue of salt. By this understand that, even though thou live among devils, God wills thee to live among them in such a way that thou look not back in thy thought at their business, but abandon them wholly, striving to keep thy soul pure and sincere with God, undisturbed by thoughts either of one thing or of another. Thou mayest take it for certain that convents and communities will never be without some occasion of stumbling, since there are never wanting devils who strive to overthrow the saints, and God permits this in order to exercise them and prove them. And if thou keep not thyself, as has been said, as though thou wert not in the house, thou canst never be a religious, however much thou doest, nor attain to holy detachment and recollection, nor free thyself from the evils that lie herein. For, if thou do not this, however good may be thy aim and however great thy zeal, the devil will entrap thee either in one place or in another, and thou art already securely entrapped when thou dost permit thy soul to be distracted in any of these ways. Remember that which is said by the apostle Saint James: 'If any man thinketh himself to be religious, bridling not his tongue, this man's religion is vain.' This is to be understood no less of inward speech than of outward. "Caution the Third," pp. 201-202.

32. See Adrian van Kaam, *On Being Yourself: Reflections on Originality and Spirituality* (Denville, N.J.: Dimension Books, Inc., 1972), pp. 47-52.

33. John 15:15.

34. John 15:26.

35. See Adrian van Kaam, "The Gentle Life Style," *Envoy*, X, II, February, 1972, pp. 25-30.

36. John 14:27.

37. John 13: 34-35.

Selected Reading List

in the

Literature of Spirituality

The Jerusalem Bible. Reader's Edition. Garden City, New York: Doubleday & Company, Inc., 1971.

The New American Bible. New York: P.J. Kenedy & Sons, 1970.

I. Literature of Traditional Catholic Spirituality

Aelred of Rievaulx. *Treatises, Pastoral Prayer.* Spencer, Mass.: Cistercian Publications, 1971.

à Kempis, Thomas. *The Imitation of Christ.* Trans. Ronald Knox and Michael Oakley. New York: Sheed and Ward, 1960.

Anonymous. *The Cloud of Unknowing.* Trans. with an Introduction by Clifton Wolters. Baltimore, Maryland: Penguin Books, 1961.

Augustine, St. *City of God.* Trans. by Gerald G. Walsh, S.J. *et. al.* New York: Image Books, 1958.

_____. *Confessions.* Trans. with an Introduction by R.S. Pine-Coffin. Baltimore, Maryland: Penguin Books, 1961.

Bernard of Clairvaux. *On the Song of Songs I.* Trans. Kilian Walsh, O.C.S.O. Spencer, Mass.: Cistercian Publications, 1971.

Brother Lawrence. *The Practice of the Presence of God.* New York: Pyramid Books, 1966.

Chautard, Jean Baptist. *The Soul of the Apostolate.* Trans. with an Introduction by Thomas Merton. Trappist, Kentucky: The Abbey of Gethsemani, 1946.

Eckhart, Meister. *A Modern Translation* by R.B. Blakney. New York: Harper & Brothers, 1957.

Francis of Assisi, St. *The Little Flowers of St. Francis.* Trans. with an Introduction by Raphael Brown. Garden City, New York: Image Books, 1958.

Francis de Sales, St. *Introduction to the Devout Life.* Trans. and ed. John K. Ryan. New York: Harper & Row, 1950.

Hilton, Walter. *The Scale of Perfection.* Trans. Gerard Sitwell. London: Burns, Oates, 1953.

Ignatius of Loyola, St. *The Spiritual Exercises of St. Ignatius.* Trans. Anthony Mottola. New York: Image Books, 1964.

John of the Cross, St. *The Complete Works of Saint John of the Cross.* Three Volumes. Trans. and ed. E. Allison Peers. Westminster, Maryland: The Newman Press, 1935.

―――――――――. *Ascent of Mount Carmel.* Trans. and ed. E. Allison Peers. Garden City, New York: Image Books, 1958.

―――――――――. *Dark Night of the Soul.* Trans. and ed. E. Allison Peers. Garden City, New York: Image Books, 1959.

―――――――――. *Spiritual Canticle.* Trans. and ed. E. Allison Peers. Garden City, New York: Image Books, 1961.

―――――――――. *Living Flame of Love.* Trans. and ed. E. Allison Peers. Garden City, New York: Image Books, 1962.

Julian of Norwich. *The Revelations of Divine Love.* Trans. James Walsh, S.J. New York: Harper & Brothers, 1961.

Libermann, Francis, C.S.Sp. *Spiritual Letters to Clergy and Religious.* Volume Two. Pittsburgh, Pa.: Duquesne University Press, 1964.

Richard of St. Victor. *Selected Writings on Contemplation.* Trans. Clare Kirchberger. London: Faber & Faber, 1957.

Rolle, Richard. *The Fire of Love.* Trans. with an Introduction by Clifton Wolters. Baltimore, Maryland: Penguin Books, 1971.

The Rule of St. Benedict. Trans. and ed Dom Justin McCann, O.S.B. London: Burns, Oates, 1921.

Teresa of Avila, St. *Complete Works of St. Teresa.* Trans. and ed. E. Allison Peers. Three Volumes.

London: Sheed and Ward, 1972 (Revised Edition).

_____. *The Life of Teresa of Jesus.* Trans. and ed. E. Allison Peers. Garden City, New York: Image Books, 1960.

_____. *Interior Castle.* Trans. and ed. E. Allison Peers. Garden City, New York: Image Books, 1961.

_____. *The Way of Perfection.* Trans. and ed. E. Allison Peers. Garden City, New York: Image Books, 1964.

Thérèse of Lisieux, St. *The Autobiography of St. Thérèse of Lisieux. The Story of a Soul.* Trans. John Beevers. Garden City, New York: Image Books, 1957.

Von Hügel, Baron Friedrich. *Letters from Baron Friedrich von Hügel to a Niece.* Ed. with an introduction by Gwendolen Green. London: J.M. Dent, 1928.

William of St. Thierry. *On Contemplating God, Prayer, Meditations.* Trans. Sister Penelope, C.S.M.V. Spencer, Mass.: Cistercian Publications, 1971.

II *Literature of Reformation Spirituality*

Brinton, Howard. *The Quaker Doctrine of Inward Peace.* Wallingford, Pa.: Pendle Hill Pamphlet, 1948.

Browne, Sir Thomas. *Religio Medici.* Ed. Jean-Jacques Denonain. Cambridge: The University Press, 1955.

Donne, John. *Devotions Upon Emergent Occasions.* Ann Arbor, Michigan: Ann Arbor Paperbacks, 1959.

_____. *Donne's Prebend Sermons.* Ed. Jane M. Mueller. Cambridge, Mass.: Harvard University Press, 1971.

_____. *The Prayers of John Donne.* Ed. Herbert H. Umbach. New Haven, Connecticut: College and University Press, 1951.

Emerson, Ralph Waldo. *Selections from Ralph Waldo Emerson.* Ed. Stephen E. Whicher. Boston: Houghton Mifflin Company, 1957.

Fox, George. *Journal.* Ed. with an Introduction by Rufus M. Jones. New York: Capricorn Books 1963.

Herbert, George. *The Poems of George Herbert.* London: Oxford University Press, 1961.

Kierkegaard, Søren. *Purity of Heart Is to Will One Thing.* Trans. Douglas V. Steere. New York: Harper & Row, 1956 (Harper Torch books).

_____ *The Prayers of Kierkegaard.* Ed. Perry D. LeFevre. Chicago: University of Chicago Press, 1956.

_____. *Training in Christianity.* Trans. Walter Lowrie. Princeton, N.J.: Princeton University Press, 1944.

———. *The Present Age.* Trans. Alexander Dru. New York: Harper & Row, 1962.

———. *Works of Love.* Trans. Howard and Edna Hong. New York: Harper & Row, 1962.

———. *Edifying Discourses.* Two Volumes. Trans. David Swenson. Minneapolis, Minnesota: Augsburg Publishing House, 1943.

———. *The Point of View for My Work as an Author.* Trans. Walter Lowrie. New York: Harper & Row, 1962 (Harper Torch books).

Lewis, C.S. *Mere Christianity.* New York: The Macmillan Company, 1960.

———. *Miracles.* New York: The Macmillan Company, 1947.

———. *Surprised by Joy.* New York: Harcourt, Brace & World, Inc., 1955.

Martz, Louis, ed. *The Meditative Poem.* New York: New York University Press, 1963.

Milton, John. *Paradise Lost and Paradise Regained.* Ed. Christopher Ricks. New York: The New American Library, 1968.

———. *Samson Agonistes.* Ed. F.T. Prince. London: Oxford University Press, 1957.

The Rule of Taizé. Taizé, France: Les Presses de Taizé, 1961.

Smith, Bradford. *Dear Gift of Life.* Wallingford, Pa.: Pendle Hill Pamphlet, 1965.

Steere, Douglas V. *On Being Present Where You Are.*

Selected Reading List in the Literature of the Spirituality

Wallingford, Pa.: Pendle Hill Pamphlet, 1967.

Taylor, Jeremy. *The Rule and Exercises of Holy Living.* Ed. Thomas S. Kepler. New York: The World Publishing Company, 1956.

──────────. *The Rule and Exercises of Holy Dying.* Ed. Thomas S. Kepler. New York: The World Publishing Company, 1952.

Thoreau, Henry David. *Walden.* Ed. Sherman Paul. Boston: Houghton Mifflin Company, 1957.

Tillich, Paul. *The Shaking of the Foundations.* New York: Charles Scribner's Sons, 1948.

──────────. *The New Being.* New York: Charles Scribner's Sons, 1955.

──────────. *The Eternal Now.* New York: Charles Scribner's Sons, 1963.

Traherne, Thomas. *Centuries, Poems, and Thanksgivings.* Ed. H.M. Margoliouth. Oxford: The Clarendon Press, 1958.

Woolman, John. *The Journal of John Woolman.* New York: Corinth Books, 1961.

III. *Literature of a Contemporary Search for Spirituality*

Anonymous. *The Way of a Pilgrim and the Pilgrim Continues His Way.* Trans. R.M. French. New York: The Seabury Press, 1965.

Bolt, Robert. *A Man for All Seasons.* New York: Random House, 1962.

Bloom, Anthony. *Beginning to Pray.* New York: Paulist Press, 1970.

Delp, Alfred, S.J. *Prison Meditations.* With an Introduction by Thomas Merton. New York: Herder and Herder, 1963.

de Saint Exupéry, Antoine. *The Little Prince.* New York: Harcourt, Brace & World, Inc., 1943.

Eliot, T.S. *The Complete Poems and Plays, 1909-1950.* New York: Harcourt, Brace & World, Inc., 1930.

_____. *Selected Poems.* New York: Harcourt Brace & World, Inc., 1934 (Harbrace Paperbound Library).

_____. *Four Quartets.* New York: Harcourt, Brace & World, Inc., 1943 (A Harvest Book).

Frank, Anne. *The Diary of a Young Girl.* New York: The Modern Library, 1952.

Godden, Rumer. *In this House of Brede.* New York: The Viking Press, 1969.

Greene, Graham. *The Heart of the Matter.* New York: The Viking Press, 1948.

_____. *The Power and the Glory.* New York: The Viking Press, 1946.

Hammarskjöld, Dag. *Markings.* Trans. Leif Sjoberg and W.H. Auden. London: Faber & Faber, 1964.

Herman, E. *Creative Prayer.* Cincinnati, Ohio: Forward Movement Publications, n.d.

Hesse, Hermann. *Siddhartha.* Trans. Hilda Rosner. New York: A New Directions Book, 1951.

——————. *Peter Camenzind.* Trans. Michael Roloff. New York: Farrar, Straus and Giroux, 1969.

Hopkins, Gerard Manley. *Poems and Prose.* Ed W.H. Gardner. Baltimore, Maryland: Penguin Books, 1953.

Houselander, Frances Caryll. *The Reed of God.* New York: Sheed and Ward, 1944.

Huxley, Aldous. *The Devils of Loudun.* New York: Harper & Row, 1952.

Kazantzakis, Nikos. *Report to Greco.* Trans. P.A. Bien. New York: Simon and Schuster, 1965.

——————. *St. Francis.* Trans. P.A. Bien. New York: Simon and Schuster, 1962.

——————. *Zorba the Greek.* Trans. Carl Wildman. New York: Simon and Schuster, 1952.

Lindbergh, Anne Morrow. *Gift from the Sea.* New York: Vintage Books, 1965.

Merton, Thomas. *The Seven Story Mountain.* New York: Harcourt, Brace & World, Inc., 1948.

——————. *No Man Is an Island.* New York: Dell Publishing Co., 1957.

——————. *Seeds of Contemplation.* Norfolk, Connecticut: New Directions, 1949.

——————. *New Seeds of Contemplation.* Norfolk, Connecticut: New Directions, 1962.

Michener, James A. *The Source.* Greenwich, Connecticut: Fawcett Publications, Inc., 1967.

Murdoch, Iris. *The Bell.* New York: Avon Books, 1966.

Paton, Alan. *Cry, the Beloved Country.* New York: Scribner, 1948.

Silone, Ignazio. *Bread and Wine.* New York: Signet Books, 1946.

van Kaam, Adrian. *On Being Involved: The Rhythm of Involvement and Detachment in Daily Life.* Denville, N.J.: Dimension Books, Inc., 1970.

——————. *On Being Yourself: Reflections on Originality and Spirituality.* Denville, N.J.: Dimension Books, Inc., 1972.

van Kaam, Adrian, Bert van Croonenburg, and Susan Muto. *The Emergent Self.* Denville, N.J.: Dimension Books, 1968.

——————. *The Participant Self.* Denville, N.J.: Dimension Books, Inc., 1969.

IV. Additional Sources: Aids to Spiritual Reading

Aulén, Gustaf. *Dag Hammarskjöld's White Book.* Philadelphia: Fortress Press, 1969.

Bouyer, Louis. *Introduction to Spirituality.* Trans. Mary Perkins Ryan. Collegeville, Minnesota: The Liturgical Press, n.d.

Boylan, Eugene, O. Cist. *This Tremendous Lover.* Westminster, Maryland: The Newman Press, 1947.

Butler, Dom Edward Cuthbert. *Western Mysticism.* Ed. David Knowles. London: Constable, 1967.

Chesterton, G.K. *Orthodoxy.* London: Fontana Books, 1961.

Selected Reading List in the Literature of the Spirituality

──────────────. *St. Francis of Assisi.* New York: Image Books, 1950.

Dessauer, Philipp. *Natural Meditation.* Trans. J. Holland Smith. New York: P.J. Kenedy & Sons, 1965.

Dewey, Bradley. *The New Obedience: Kierkegaard on Imitating Christ.* Washington, D.C.: Corpus Books, 1968.

Eliade, Mircea. *The Sacred and the Profane.* New York: Harcourt, Brace & World, Inc., 1959.

Gilson, Etienne. *The Mystical Theology of St. Bernard.* Trans. A.H.C. Downes. London: Sheed and Ward, 1940.

Inge, W.R. *Mysticism in Religion.* London: Rider & Company, 1969.

James, William. *The Varieties of Religious Experience.* New York: The New American Library, 1958.

Johnston, William, S.J. *The Mysticism of the Cloud of Unknowing.* New York: Desclee Company, 1967.

──────────────. *The Still Point.* New York, Fordham University Press, 1970.

Jones, Rufus M. *Spiritual Reformers in the 16th and 17th Centuries.* Boston: Beacon Press, 1959.

Knowles, Dom David. *The English Mystics.* London: Burns, Oates, 1927.

──────────────. *The English Mystical Tradition.* New York: Harper, 1961.

Knox, Ronald. *Enthusiasm.* New York: Oxford University Press, 1961.

Lavelle, Louis. *The Meaning of Holiness.* New York: Pantheon Books, Inc., 1954.

Leclercq, Dom Jean. *The Love of Learning and the Desire for God.* Trans. Catharine Misrahi. New York: Fordham University Press, 1961.

Marechal, Joseph. *Studies in the Psychology of the Mystics.* Trans. Algar Thorold. Albany: Magi Books, 1964.

McGinley, Phyllis. *Saint-Watching.* New York: The Viking Press, 1971.

Merton, Thomas. *Mystics and Zen Masters.* New York: A Delta Book, 1969.

——————. *Zen and the Birds of Appetite.* New York: A New Directions Book, 1968.

——————. *Spiritual Direction and Meditation.* Collegeville, Minnesota: The Liturgical Press, 1960.

Otto, Rudolf. *The Idea of the Holy.* Trans. John W. Harvey. New York: Oxford University Press, 1958.

Pourrat, Pierre. *Christian Spirituality.* Westminster, Maryland: Newman, 1953.

Ricoeur, Paul. *The Symbolism of Evil.* New York: Harper & Row, 1967.

Rohrbach, Peter-Thomas, O.C.D. *Conversation with Christ: An Introduction to Mental Prayer.* Chicago: Fides Publishers Association, 1956.

Selected Reading List in the Literature of the Spirituality

Sertillanges, A.D., O.P. *The Intellectual Life.* Trans. Mary Ryan. Cork: The Mercier Press, 1948.

Underhill, Evelyn. *Mysticism.* New York: A Dutton Paperback, 1961.

——————. *Practical Mysticism.* New York: A Dutton Paperback, 1915.

van Croonenburg, Bert. *Don't Be Discouraged.* Denville, N.J.: Dimension Books, Inc., 1972.

van Kaam, Adrian. *A Light to the Gentiles.* Denville, N.J.: Dimension Books, Inc., 1959.

——————. *Religion and Personality.* Englewood Cliffs, N.J.: Prentice-Hall, Inc., 1964.

——————. *Personality Fulfillment in the Spiritual Life.* Denville, N.J.: Dimension Books, Inc., 1966.

——————. *Personality Fulfillment in the Religious Life.* Denville, N.J.: Dimension Books, Inc., 1968.

——————. *The Vowed Life.* Denville, N.J.: Dimension Books, Inc., 1968.

——————. *Envy and Originality.* Garden City, New York: Doubleday & Company, Inc., 1972.

van Zeller, Hubert. *The Holy Rule.* New York: Sheed and Ward, 1958.

Worden, Thomas. *The Psalms are Christian Prayer.* New York: Sheed and Ward, 1961.